Written with a deft touch and plenty of hu
fills each compact chapter with enough ne
tertain even a 35-year resident like myself.
appeal as much (if not more) to locals.
        —Judy Irving, Producer-Dir

The perfect go-to book for those who live in, love, and host visitors to our city. Chock full of answers to questions you didn't even know you had.
        —David Perry, Board member, San Francisco Museum and Historical Society

Art Peterson has provided us with a precious gift—enjoyable, easy to read bites of San Francisco, written with humor, clarity, and style.
        —Ruth Gottstein, publisher of Masha Zakheim's
        Coit Tower San Francisco Its History and Art

Art Peterson brings to *Why Is That Bridge Orange?* the same talent for engaging and succinct story telling he has long demonstrated as a teacher, writer, and editor.
        —Sharon J. Washington, Executive Director, National Writing Project

Why Is That Bridge Orange? is one of a kind. This book brings together an incredible variety of San Francisco experience and tells the story of one of the greatest cities of the world in a way that is lively, educational, and entertaining.
        —David Chiu, President, San Francisco Board of Supervisors.

Like its infamous Lombard "Crooked" Street, San Francisco is a town of many twists and turns. Art Peterson examines many of these quirks and curiosities and engagingly tells how they came to be.
        —Jeff Adachi, SF Public Defender

Read this book immediately, so you will sound smart and knowledgeable when your out-of-town guests ask tough questions about our glorious town.
        —Daniel Handler, Author of Lemony Snickett's *A Series of Unfortunate Events*

As a city boy and non-fiction writer focusing on North Beach history, my first reaction to this book was "Dang, why didn't I think of that?" Art Peterson answers questions that have lingered in my mind for years and provides a history and guide that is hard to put down.
        —Dick Boyd, Author of *Broadway North Beach: The Golden Years*

Art Peterson brings into perspective San Francisco's roguish and delightful past by taking a close and well-photographed look at the monuments that are still with us.

—**Denise D'Anne, Labor and Environmental Activist**

I've been researching San Francisco history for a long time but still got caught up in *Why Is That Bridge Orange?* The book is a great and compact summary of some of San Francisco's most interesting tales. For visitors, it's a good and reliable guide that offers views beyond the usual tourist spots.

—**Julie Christensen, Community Leader**

This is what a book about a city should be. *Why Is That Bridge Orange?* brings the then and now together in rich detail with uncluttered execution. Highly readable text, wonderful photos, overall enchanting.

—**Mal Sharpe, Legendary Bay Area Radio Performer, Humorist and Director of the "Big Money in Jazz Band"**

This is anything but a book of San Francisco Trivial Pursuit. Art Peterson, a skilled storyteller, masterfully weaves little known tales of San Francisco's past into entertaining and informative vignettes. I'll never see the city the same way again.

—**Grant Faulkner, Executive Director National Story Month and Founder of "100 Word Stories"**

A perfect blend of history, mystery, and great photography.

—**Catherine Accardi, Author of** *San Francisco's North Beach and Telegraph Hill* **and** *San Francisco Landmarks*

From the quirky to the profound, from then to the now, *Why Is That Bridge Orange?* covers scores of quintessentially important aspects of our amazing city. It encapsulates all that makes San Francisco the envy of the world.

—**Aaron Peskin, President, San Francisco Board of Supervisors 2005-2009**

San Francisco's charms and endless fascinations come to life in this enthralling page turner. Even longtime San Franciscans will learn a lot from it.

—**Timothy Ferris, Longtime San Franciscan and Author of** *Coming of Age in the Milky Way*

Why Is That Bridge Orange? lifts the curtain on the secrets that make San Francisco San Francisco, pursuing the city's secret stories, unlikely dreams, and zany tales.

—**Jon Golinger, Past President Telegraph Hill Dwellers, and Chairman, The Committee to Save Coit Tower**

Why Is That Bridge Orange?

San Francisco for the Curious

By Art Peterson

Inquiring Minds Productions

For Carol

Publisher's Cataloging-in-Publication

Peterson, Art, 1933–

Why is That Bridge Orange? : San Francisco for the Curious

by Art Peterson.

pages cm

Includes bibliographical references and index.

ISBN-13: 978-0-926664-19-7

ISBN-10: 0-926664-19-0

1. San Francisco (Calif.)—Miscellanea. I. Title.

   F869.S34P48 2013   979.4'61
               QBI13-600163

Editors: William Pates and LisaRuth Elliott

Book design and production: Chris Carlsson

Front cover photo Richard Zimmerman (richard@rezphotos.com)
Back cover photo by Chris Carlsson
Cartography by Ben Pease, Pease Press Maps (www.peasepress.com)

Printed in China.

Table of Contents

INTRODUCTION 5

1. Phillip Burton 9

2. Transamerica Pyramid 11

3. How Does a Cable Car Work? 14

4. San Francisco Sourdough Bread 17

5. Alcatraz 19

6. Bison in Golden Gate Park 22

7. The Sing Chong Building 25

8. The Double Play—Seal's Stadium ... 27

9. The Vaillancourt Fountain 31

10. John McLaren 33

11. Alma Spreckels 35

12. The Murphy Windmill 38

13. Neiman Marcus/City of Paris 41

14. Japanese Tea Garden 45

15. The Palace of Fine Arts 47

16. Room 1221—Hotel St. Francis 50

17. Balmy Alley 53

18. The Old Ship Saloon 55

19. Earthquake Cottages 58

20. V. C. Morris Building—
    140 Maiden Lane 60

21. Classic Ferries 62

22. Columbus Tower 65

23. Bay to Breakers 68

24. Cameron House 70

25. Burritt Alley 73

26. The Grand Staircase at City Hall ... 75

27. Telegraph Hill 79

28. Pioneer Monument 81

29. Doggie Diner Head 84

30. Colombo Market Arch 86

31. Why are San Francisco Fire Hydrants
    Different Colors? 89

32. Patty Hearst's Hideout 92

33. Coit Tower 95

34. Coit Tower Murals 98

35. Philo T. Farnsworth 101

36. Why Is the Golden Gate Bridge
    Painted Orange? 104

37. The East Side of Telegraph Hill ... 106

38. The Columbarium 109

39. Why Are All Those Flags in Front of
    the Fairmont Hotel? 111

40. Angel Island Immigration Station 113

41. Harvey Milk 116

42. Grace Cathedral 119

43. Harding Park 122

44. Fontana East and West 124

45. Harry Bridges Plaza 126

46. Kezar Stadium Gate 129

6

47. Emperor Norton 131

48. *Transcendence* at A. P. Giannini
     Plaza 134

49. The Embarcadero Freeway 137

50. St. Francis of Assisi 140

51. Stevenson Monument 142

52. Fort Point 145

53. Palace of the Legion of Honor ... 148

54. Why Does San Francisco Weather
     Change From One Block
     to the Next? 150

55. Joseph B. Strauss 152

56. San Francisco's Pride Parade 154

57. How Does One Celebrate
     Chinese New Year? 156

58. How Does the Mission District's
     Cinco de Mayo Celebration
     Differ from its Carnival? 158

59. The International Hotel 160

60. Lotta's Fountain 163

61. Why is Lombard Street
     So Crooked? 166

62. San Francisco Armory 168

63. Levi's 171

64. The Barbary Coast Hippodrome . 173

65. San Francisco Topless Dancing 176

66. George Moscone 179

67. How Do You Get a Street Named
     After You in San Francisco? 182

68. Steam Beer 184

69. Woodward's Garden 186

70. Mary Ellen Pleasant's Trees 188

71. Sun Yat-sen 191

72. Treasure Island 193

73. Why Are There Parrots
     on Telegraph Hill? 196

74. Why Are San Francisco Summers
     Cold and Foggy? 199

75. The Cross at the Peak of
     Mount Davidson 200

76. The Martini 203

77. Tadich Grill: The Original Cold
     Day Restaurant 204

78. The Tenderloin 207

79. William Ralston 208

80. The Sutro Baths 210

81. The Lions of Sutro Heights 212

82. The Audiffred Building 214

83. Sutro Tower 216

84. Bloody Thursday Commemoration
     Mural/Sculpture 218

85. Hearst Building 220

86. Playland at the Beach 223

ABOUT THE AUTHOR 226

PHOTO CREDITS 227

BIBLIOGRPAHY 229

INDEX 233

Introduction

The idea for *Why Is That Bridge Orange?* came to me one day when I was picking weeds from my little garden in front of my home, 100 yards from Coit Tower. This day, as always, passing tourists were bursting with questions "How did those parrots get here?" "What is this for?" (referring to Coit Tower looming above), "Why is this called Telegraph Hill?"

I thought, "You know, many people who live here have similar questions—Why is the Golden Gate Bridge painted orange? Why is Lombard Street crooked? Why are there bison in Golden Gate Park?" I had an idea for a project to help quench this thirst for answers to questions about our glorious surroundings. I would write a book that takes a close look at the elements of San Francisco that natives and tourists encounter daily.

I resolved to consider topics as diverse as the Palace of Fine Arts and sourdough bread, placing each in its historical context, telling their stories with the vitality they deserved.

This is a book for San Franciscans, who love the city and its lore and want to become more familiar with the living history they experience everyday, and for newcomers, who may find in this book an introduction to their new environment. Visitors—whose stay is often far too brief—will be able to take away a visual, informative reminder of their San Francisco experience.

As a lifelong Bay Area resident, I have been itching to write a book like this for decades. I now have a chance to share with others something of the back story of one of the earth's special places.

Map 1

TIBURON

Angel Island

40

SAUSALITO

101 1

Marin Headlands

San Francisco Bay

Alcatraz

5

Golden Gate

36

Treasure Island

72

See Map 2

52
55

Yerba Buena Island

80

15 **79**

Richardson Marina

Presidio **19** **35** Cow Hollow

Lombard
Union Broadway

Bay

Columbus
Montgomery
Embarcadero

Van Ness

Pacific Heights California Downtown

53 Sea Cliff

80

80

Point Lobos

81

86

6

Lincoln

Washington

101

1

California
Arguello

SAN FRANCISCO

Geary

Western Addition Civic
Center Market Harrison

25th Ave Geary **4**

Richmond **38**

Fulton **10**

34th Ave Park Presidio Blvd

Masonic
Divisadero
Fillmore

8th
6th

King

3rd

Hayes
Oak

South of
Market

Mission Bay

14

Golden Gate Park

12

Lincoln Way

Irving Inner **46**
Sunset

Judah

Stanyan Fell

Haight Haight
Ashbury

Cole 17th

Duboce

Dolores

16th
Mission
Bryant

20th Potrero
Hill

Sunset **54**

9th Ave 19th Ave

Castro **18th**

31 Church **58**

Mission 24th **17** Cesar

74

Noriega

83

Noe Valley

Chavez

Forest
Hill

Market Castro

101 280

Portola

Parkside Taraval

1

West
Portal

Diamond
Heights

30th

Bernal
Heights
Cortland

Evans

Sloat

St Francis
Wood

75

Glen
Park

San Jose

Bayview

Oakdale

3rd

29

46th Ave

Great Hwy

Lake

43

Merced

Westwood
Park
Ocean

Sunnyside
Monterey

Juniper Serra

Phelan

280

Silver

Portola

Bayshore Blvd

San Bruno

Hunters Point

Ingleside

San Jose
Alemany

Persia

Excelsior

Mission Geneva

Mansell

Visitation Valley

101

Oceanview

Crocker-Amazon

280

Pacific Ocean

35 Skyline

John Daly

1 280 Mission

DALY CITY

N

0   1 Mile

Map 2

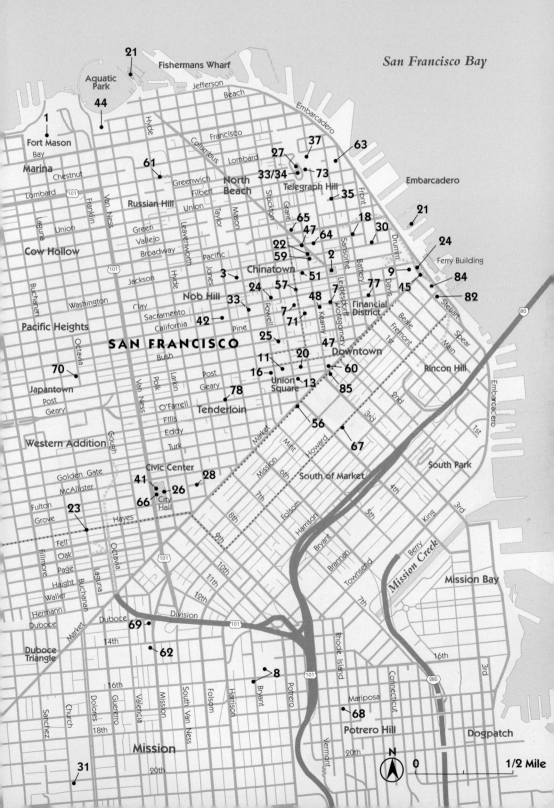

San Francisco Bay

21 Fishermans Wharf

Aquatic Park

44

Jefferson

Beach

Embarcadero

1

Fort Mason

Bay

Francisco

37

63

Marina

Chestnut

61

Lombard

27

Embarcadero

Lombard

Greenwich

North Beach

33/34

73

Franklin

Van Ness

Russian Hill

Filbert

Telegraph Hill

35

Cow Hollow

Union

Green

Vallejo

Broadway

Pacific

65

18

21

Laguna

Leavenworth

Taylor

Mason

Stockton

47

64

30

24

Ferry Building

Buchanan

Jackson

Hyde

Jones

3

Chinatown

22

59

2

Sansome

Battery

Drumm

9

Davis

84

Washington

Clay

Nob Hill

33

24

57

51

48

Leidesdorff

Montgomery

77

45

82

Pacific Heights

Sacramento

California

42

25

Pine

7

71

Kearny

Financial District

Beale

Fremont

1st

Steuart

Spear

SAN FRANCISCO

Bush

11

20

47

Downtown

Rincon Hill

70

Octavia

Larkin

16

Union Square

13

60

85

Japantown

Post

Geary

Polk

Van Ness

Post

Geary

78

Tenderloin

Main

2nd

Rincon Hill

Western Addition

O'Farrell

Ellis

Eddy

Turk

56

67

South Park

Golden Gate

McAllister

Civic Center

41

28

Howard

9th

South of Market

4th

3rd

Fulton

Grove

23

66

26

City Hall

Hayes

8th

Folsom

5th

King

Berry

Mission Bay

Fell

Oak

Page

Haight

Waller

Octavia

Buchanan

Laguna

Hayes

9th

10th

11th

Harrison

Bryant

Brannan

Townsend

7th

Mission Creek

3rd

Hermann

Duboce

Market

Duboce

69

Division

Rhode Island

16th

3rd

Duboce Triangle

14th

62

Folsom

Potrero

Mariposa

Connecticut

Dogpatch

Church

Sanchez

Dolores

Guerrero

Valencia

Mission

South Van Ness

Folsom

Harrison

Bryant

8

68

Potrero Hill

16th

Mission

18th

Vermont

20th

N

0   1/2 Mile

31

20th

Who's This?

1. Phillip Burton

This is Phillip Burton, the one-time congressman from San Francisco, who, in 1972, pushed through the legislation that created the 80,000-acre Golden Gate National Recreation Area that serves 7 million Bay Area residents today. As may be clear enough from this representation of the man at Fort Mason, Burton was not a great outdoorsman himself. His biographer John Jacobs writes, he "was less at home in Muir Woods than in a darkened cocktail lounge with an unfiltered Chesterfield in one hand and a tumbler of Stoli in the other."

A personal indifference to nature, however, did not make him any less responsive to the conservationists in his constituency, who, from the mid-1960s on, had been sounding the alarm about the perils of urban sprawl. Several factors were coming together to threaten the continued existence of Bay Area open space. A growing and more prosperous population needed housing, and the U.S. Army—which had acquired large parcels of land in the area for coastal defense—was eager to get rid of property that had become a white elephant. Developers were ready to pounce. Marincello, a development of 50 apartment buildings housing 25,000 people, was to be located on the Marin Headlands southwest of the Golden Gate Bridge.

Meanwhile, environmentalists, led by the Sierra Club, were cobbling together a bill that would give urban residents, many without the means to hop in the family car for a two-week excursion to Yellowstone, a green place of their own. Burton, who was chairman of the House Subcommittee on National Parks, was very much on board. When he met with Edgar Wayburn of the Sierra Club he asked him why he hadn't included a particular parcel in the proposed park boundaries. Wayburn replied, "I didn't think it would be politically feasible." Burton answered, "You tell me what you want, not what's politically feasible." Wayburn came back with an expanded plan that Burton, using his skills as a coalition builder and vote counter, indeed, made feasible.

Even President Richard Nixon was eager to get on board, making a hurried trip to the Bay Area in advance of the 1972 election. "Nixon to dedicate uncreated park," the *San Francisco Chronicle* headline read.

When the bill passed, Burton waxed uncharacteristically poetic: "Here a man can walk and be lost in peace, hearing the sea, feeling the wind touching the land." Jacobs says that Burton would be as likely to be that man he described as "he would be found taking LSD in a Berkeley commune."

Parks, of course, were far from Burton's only legislative interest. He used his unflagging energy to push for workers' safety, coal miners' protection, farm workers' rights, AIDS research, and many other causes to benefit ordinary folks.

His success came at least as much from the pleasure he took in the political game as in the nobleness of his causes. Once when reminiscing with a fellow politician about issues surrounding the Golden Gate National Recreation Area, he mentioned "a thing of beauty." "The place does have some lovely features," his colleague said. "Not the park," Burton said, "the bill."

How Did This Get Built?

2. The Transamerica Pyramid

At the time of its completion in 1972, the Transamerica Pyramid at the corner of Washington and Montgomery Streets had few advocates. The structure, a present-day icon almost as representative of San Francisco as the Golden Gate Bridge and the cable cars, was called "inhuman" (and that by the city's planning director!) and an "abomination" by the *Chronicle's* architectural critic.

There was no question that the building was more than a little bit out of scale. The Transamerica Corporation decided that its three-story wedding cake of a structure across the street at Columbus and Montgomery—now home to the Church of Scientology—was no longer in keeping with the image of the multibillion-dollar global conglomerate that it had become. It proposed a 1,000-foot-high building in an area where city zoning called for a 65-foot height limit. The architect of the structure was to be William Pereira, whose previous contribution to the San Francisco skyline had been the Fairmont Hotel annex tower—a work that by most objective standards would inspire little confidence in the architect's aesthetic judgment.

The corporation, hell bent on constructing the tallest building west of the Mississippi, began a vigorous lobbying campaign, even hiring, according to Peter Booth Wiley, hippies to picket while carrying signs reading "Artists for the Pyramid." The moving force behind the construction of the building was Mayor Joseph Alioto, who liked to think of San Francisco as a European city. In his mind, the Transamerica Pyramid was to be our Eiffel Tower. A hugely successful antitrust attorney, Alioto directed his powers of persuasion toward the Planning Commission and won approval for construction of the building by a narrow vote. The city even handed over a part of Merchant Street to advance the corporation's plan.

The eventual size and shape of the building was the result of push and pull compromises. In response to community pressure, the height of the building was reduced to 853 feet, the top 211 feet of which was to be an uninhabited aluminum spire. The triangular shape of the building was, it was hoped, both a way of reducing the potential shadow cast by a blockbuster building and cutting back on the square footage to bring it closer into compliance with the city's height-to-bulk guidelines.

Those interested in observing the construction of the building can rent a copy of the 2007 film *Zodiac* that presents a time-lapse computer-generated version of the building as it went up between 1969 and 1971. In fact, the building has been cast in several supporting movie roles, most notably in the 1978 remake of *Invasion of the Body Snatchers* in which it becomes a visual motif. The Transamerica Corporation was tied to United Artists at the time, the company that made the movie, thus making the pyramid one of the most conspicuous examples of product placement in film history.

3. How Does a Cable Car Work?

Like many technological innovations of the Victorian Era, the idea for the cable car that surveyor and bridge builder Andrew Hallidie bestowed on the city of San Francisco in 1873 was a model of durable simplicity. Hallidie is said to have been prodded toward his invention after viewing the sad spectacle of overburdened horses slipping and sliding and even dying pulling trolleys up San Francisco's hills. His invention very much caught on. Before the 1906 earthquake and fire there were 600 cable cars trundling around town on more than 100 miles of track. The system is now reduced to three lines and 40 cars, but the basic elements of Hallidie's creation are very much in place today.

The four cables that propel the system's remaining lines are all driven by a single motor in the cable car barn at Washington and Mason Streets. Housed here are enormous pulleys, around which the cables wind, pulling at a speed of 9.4 miles per hour. The gripman (an occupational designation that after 1998 would include the first woman operator, Fannie Mae Barnes) attaches a pliers-like device that holds the cable tight in a pair of wooden jaws. To halt the car the operator merely disengages this device and applies the brakes. Things get a bit hairy on the curves where a series of horizontal pulleys break the curve up into short sections around which the cable rolls. At Mason Street and Columbus Avenue, for example, there are 93 separate pulleys. While the cable car mechanism has kept the cars rolling smoothly along, the cars' continued existence has traveled a rocky road. In 1947, the golden age of the internal-combustion engine hit San Francisco and then Mayor Roger Lapham and the Board of Supervisors were poised to replace all the cable cars with buses. (Perhaps not the best idea in what was at the time known as a "clutch and brake" town.)

However, Lapham and his colleagues had not counted on the organizational skills of San Francisco matron Friedel Klussman, the "cable car lady." Klussman believed that there "was nothing more terrifying to politicians than a delegation of women marching up the steps of City Hall." She organized just such a march to save the cable cars. When that effort did not have the desired effect, she orchestrated a ballot initiative to accomplish this feat. The initiative passed overwhelmingly.

In 1964, the cable cars were designated as the country's only moving national landmark.

1LB
SOURDOUGH ROUND

$3.99

Who Thought of....?

4. San Francisco Sourdough Bread

An old San Francisco joke goes:

Customer: "Do you sell sourdough?"

Grocer: "We haven't had any complaints so far."

True enough. The complaints against San Francisco sourdough bread are few and far between. Residents love their sourdough.

Bragging rights for the creation of this everyday delicacy can be traced to the arrival in San Francisco in 1849 of baker Isadore Boudin and his family from the small French town of Champiny-sur-Yonne in the Bourgogne region. It wasn't that Boudin invented the generic sourdough. The technique for creating this bread had been around since the ancient Egyptians. Essentially all one needs to make this bread is a "starter" that's a mixture of grain and liquid (usually flour and water) that is left out to be inhabited by so-called wild yeast (different than today's commercially produced yeast)—and bacteria. This concoction puts even the amateur baker well on the way to a loaf of sourdough.

During the 1849 California Gold Rush, most every miner packed along a starter as a guarantee of sustenance in the rugged Sierra foothills. In fact, miners, returning to the city from a tour in the Sierra, would often be referred to as "sourdoughs."

What Boudin did, though, was to bring to this rudimentary sourdough technique the special secrets of French baking. He devised a golden loaf that was crispy and chewy on the outside and airy light and springy on the inside. It was also more sour than other sourdough breads. Boudin wasn't alone in exploiting early San Franciscans' love of bread. By 1853, San Francisco, with a population of about 50,000, had 53 bakeries, many baking sourdough from starters of which some are still in use today.

Boudin and his fellow bakers cannot take full credit for the delicious bread baked in San Francisco. Much of the bread's distinctive flavor results from the city's ecosystem. Here the bacteria gel is not like that which occurs in other places. Something is in the air here, not least of which is the fog. There is a story of a baker who disassembled his plant, transported its pieces along with his recipes to Iowa, and set up a cookie-cutter version of what he had in San Francisco. Alas, the outcome had nothing to do with San Francisco sourdough.

What was missing was that special quality in the starter, *Lactobacillus sanfranciscensis*—as the food chemists elegantly put it.

Additionally, there is something else quirky about San Francisco sourdough. On warm days the bread rises faster, on foggy, humid days, slower. This produces a variety in taste. The final step in production is to shape and score the bread by hand giving it its distinctive ridges. This means that like snowflakes, no loaf is exactly like any other. Still, for more than a century, local sourdough aficionados have willingly taken their chances.

Why is This There?

5. Alcatraz

Alcatraz Federal Penitentiary was located in the middle of the Bay, according to the Bureau of Prisons, because no convict would have a chance to escape the island. In 1934, the former military prison was converted into what was advertised as an "escape proof" bastion for the 1,554 "incorrigibles" who were housed there over a 30-year period.

The bureau had good reason for its confidence. The chilly water and treacherous tides of San Francisco Bay did not invite aquatic adventure. As well, there were the constant shakedowns, bed checks, body searches and patrols that left the cons little breathing room.

That's not to say that a few inmates didn't try to make a break for it. The bloodiest of these efforts was a 1946 getaway attempt in which three of the six men who attempted the escape, and several guards ended up dead. The cons figured out a way to get to the guns located in the caged-off gun gallery. After clubbing guards, taking their keys, and tossing the guards into a vacant cell, the inmates headed for the prison yard, but—bad luck—they didn't have the right key. Panicking, in an apparent attempt to cover their tracks, they returned to the cell where they had stashed the guards and began shooting them at point-blank range. Incredibly, some lived and scrawled the name of the escapees on the cell wall.

The Marines and National Guard were brought in for a two-day assault, and in the end three men were returned to their cells—two of them later to die in the gas chamber at San Quentin.

For years after this explosive scenario, relative calm reigned at the prison until a June day in 1962 when a more cerebral bunch conceived an escape plan. Stealing spoons from the mess hall, the cons sharpened them and worked every day after lockup to enlarge an air vent on the back wall of their cells beneath their sinks. They used these escape hatches to reach a crawl space leading to a wire mesh cage on the roof of the prison where they fashioned a raft made of old raincoats—following instructions in a book about raft making stolen from the prison library. On the night of the escape, in their beds they left papier-mâché dummy heads topped with human hair from the prison barber shop. They made it past manned gun towers, 12-foot fences topped with barbed wire and spotlights, all the while lugging their raft which they successfully launched. Their plan was to reach Angel Island or Marin County and head north, staying away from San Francisco.

Did they make it? Almost no one these days thinks so. The belief is that all three drowned. However, the Herculean effort of these men did call attention to the decrepit condition of the prison, which was closed forever a year later in 1963.

Today, of course, we know it is no great trick to "escape" from Alcatraz, wet suits optional. San Francisco's South End Rowing Club sponsors an annual Alcatraz Invitational Swim; each year, there's an "Escape from Alcatraz Triathlon" that draws 2,000 participants. In May 2006, Braxton Bilbrey, a 7-year-old second-grader from Glendale, Arizona, made the 1.4-mile swim from Alcatraz to Aquatic Park in 47 minutes.

Why Are Those There?

6. Bison in Golden Gate Park

The answer to this one reflects well on San Francisco as a progressive city. In 1891, long before there was an Endangered Species Act, the city, pushed by Park Superintendent John McLaren, set out to save the bison (or buffalo as they are colloquially known). McLaren brought to Golden Gate Park from the plains of Wyoming a majestic exemplar of the species to take its place among the bears, elk, and goats that roamed free in the park at the time. The animal was given the name Ben Harrison after Benjamin Harrison, then president of the United States. Ben was soon joined by a female companion, Sarah Bernhardt, named after the great turn-of-the-century actress. Ben and Sarah soon did what boy and girl bison do, and the San Francisco herd, now located in the park on John F. Kennedy Drive just east of 41st Avenue, was on its way.

It was not a moment too soon. In 1800, 50 million bison populated the American plains. By 1890, there were only 800 left. Slaughtered indiscriminately by white hunters, the beasts were often killed for their tongues, considered a delicacy in the 19th century. The construction of the transcontinental railroad upped the ante. Buffalo Bill, working as a hunter killing bison to feed railway workers, bragged of causing the demise of 4,200 bison in a 17-month period. When the railroad was completed, the trains would often halt when a herd was spotted so passengers could engage in target practice, leaving the carcasses to rot.

San Francisco, however, was providing a counterweight to these destructive practices. Ben Harrison was joined by other presidential namesakes such as Grover Cleveland, Bill McKinley, and other buffalo imported from Yellowstone National Park. By 1918, the San Francisco paddock showcased 30 bison. Over the years, the herd has been decimated by disease and death. (A domesticated bison lives about 25 years.) When tuberculosis struck the herd in the 1980s, seven of its members were quarantined at a pasture adjacent to San Francisco's County Jail in San Bruno, where a coordinated escape attempt failed. More recently a young calf died after running into a fence in an effort to escape an unleashed and pursuing dog.

The herd has periodically been replenished, however, by the city and by private donors. For bison in general, things are not nearly as gloomy as they were in 1891. In 1903, the federal government banned the slaughter of these animals. Now more than a century later, 350,000 of this species live (if not exactly roam) in the United States. The herd in Golden Gate Park, which has birthed a good 500 calves, has made a proud contribution to this renaissance.

Why Is This There?

7. The Sing Chong Building

The name of the prosperous businessman Look Tin Eli may not get much attention in the annals of San Francisco, but we can thank his sure-footed intervention after the 1906 earthquake and fire for the Sing Chong Building at California Street and Grant Avenue and for the other graceful-if-faux-Chinese structures that dot Chinatown today.

The buildings of the Chinese community that had spread out on the 22 square blocks around Portsmouth Square after 1850 were flattened in the catastrophic events of 1906, and the 15,000 Chinese residents were scattered to Golden Gate Park, the Presidio, and Oakland. This forced diaspora made the city fathers very happy. For many years, the powers that be had been trying to find a way to remove the Chinese from this very valuable real estate in the heart of San Francisco. The presence of this "foreign" race entrenched on such a prime location stuck in the craw of many white-skinned residents. The Chinese were "The Other." They were perceived as dirty and diseased. Their Streets emitted a thousand smells. The women had bound feet, the men wore their hair in queues. They were the proprietors of brothels and opium dens and sometimes the men married white women.

So the destruction of Chinatown was, for the white community, the up side of the earthquake and fire. The *Overland Monthly* summed up the exhilaration: "Fire has reclaimed to civilization and cleanliness the Chinese ghetto...." God in his "divine wisdom" had chosen some of his targets carefully.

A committee of civic leaders was formed to relocate the Chinese. Prominent citizens, who otherwise were not speaking to each other, united under the banner of racism. They thought they had found the perfect spot for the forced migration: Hunters Point at the south end of the city, home to slaughterhouses and murky swamps. Needless to say, the Chinese lacked enthusiasm for this plan, and even the government of China got involved. The Empress Dowager, head of the Chinese government, said she intended to rebuild the Chinese consulate at its previous location, right in the heart of Chinatown. An international incident was brewing.

That's when Look Tin Eli got involved. Why not, he asked, create a dreamscape Chinatown that would draw on visions of the Mysterious Orient that Caucasians carried about in their heads? The San Francisco Real Estate Board loved the idea: "Whereas . . . the Chinese style of architecture will make it picturesque and attractive to tourists [we] recommend to all property owners, to have their buildings rebuilt with fronts of Oriental and artistic appearance."

Look Tin Eli went to work. He picked up loans from Hong Kong and hired white architects to ensure he was getting the Orient filtered through Caucasian eyes. The Sing Chong Building, for instance, is an Edwardian structure with a ground-floor retail establishment, but topped with a sort of Chinese pagoda. A pagoda in China is strictly about religion. But Look Tin Eli's renaissance worked. By 1908, the Chinatown population was again at 15,000. Today, 70,000 residents live in the largest Chinatown outside of Asia. Chinese are no longer ghettoized and contribute to every aspect of San Francisco life. Look Tin Eli's fake, but charming, buildings are still around, one more reminder of Chinese resilience.

8. The Double Play—Seals Stadium

This sign that fronts the Double Play bar at 16th and Bryant Streets is the only reminder of the storied beginnings of the San Francisco Giants that in 1958 moved into Seals Stadium across the street. The stadium with its 2,600 bleacher seats was appropriately described by sportscaster Russ Hodges as that "beautiful little watch charm of a ballpark." Now the site of a shopping center, the stadium was home to the legendary San Francisco Seals. Old-time residents will remember the excitement when New York Giants owner Horace Stoneham brought his losing team to San Francisco in 1958. The on-again, off-again club had finished sixth in an eight-team league two years in a row. Its home field—The Polo Grounds—was about to be demolished and attendance was half what it used to be.

Spurred on by the news that Brooklyn Dodgers owner Walter O'Malley would be moving his team to Los Angeles, then San Francisco Mayor George Christopher goaded Stoneham into bringing his team to the 18,600 seat stadium where the Seals had performed before adoring fans. It was as a San Francisco Seal that the young Joe DiMaggio perfected his craft, in 1933 hitting successfully in 61 straight games for the Pacific Coast League team.

Arriving in town with one superstar, the already legendary Willie Mays, the Giants began beefing up the team with players fans still celebrate today: Orlando Cepeda, Willie McCovey, and pitcher Juan Marichal, he of the high leg kick and intimidating delivery.

By 1962, after moving into the now much demeaned, but then celebrated Candlestick Park, the Giants were ready to play serious ball. That year, with seven games to play, the team was behind the Dodgers, four games out of first place. By season's end they had pulled even with L.A. and then proceeded to defeat the despised Southlanders in a three-game playoff series. Then it was on to the World Series.

That series against the Yankees is remembered by fans for what might have been.

It came down to a tiebreaking game seven, a pitchers' duel in which the Yankees were up 1-0 when the Giants came to bat in the bottom of the ninth. With two outs, Mays was on second with McCovey at bat. A hard line drive—a sure hit off pitcher Ralph Terry—brought the fans to their feet. Terry threw

down his glove in disgust. But second baseman Bobby Richardson had moved out of position chasing a previous McCovey foul ball and was at the wrong place at the right time. Richardson snagged the ball, robbing McCovey of the game-changing hit, giving the Yankees the series.

The mourning began. In December 1962, *Peanuts* creator and Giants' fan Charles Schulz had Linus and Charlie Brown sitting on a porch looking glum for three panels. In the fourth, Charlie reaches toward the heavens. "Why couldn't McCovey have hit the ball just three feet higher?" he laments. Unfortunately, Charlie was only around in reprints when his heroes redeemed themselves with World Series victories in 2010 and 2012.

Seals Stadium

What's This?

9. The Vaillancourt Fountain

This 1971 structure, known to San Franciscans as the Vaillancourt Fountain, has not been universally loved. To the late *Chronicle* architecture critic Alan Temko, for instance, it resembled nothing so much as the droppings of a giant dog with square intestines. Other rather more sympathetic viewers see it as a very beautiful sewage outlet.

The creator of the work was the French Canadian politically engaged sculptor Armand Vaillancourt, who spent five years on the design and execution of this 40-foot-high, 710-foot-long work. On the night before the fountain's dedication, he anonymously christened the piece with his own hand, scrawling "*Québec Libre!*"—Free Quebec!—on one of the fountains protuberances.

By the next morning, the graffiti had been removed. The vandal remained shadowy until, during the dedication ceremony, Vaillancourt emerged from the waters and began replicating his handiwork of the night before, this time explaining he was not defacing his sculpture, but making a "joyous statement." "This fountain," he said, "is dedicated to all freedom—Free Quebec! Free East Pakistan, Free Vietnam. Free the whole world."

His local sponsors were not amused, and the sculptor left town in a hurry as furious protesters passed out leaflets attacking his work as a "howling obscenity" and a "perfidious eyesore."

Over the years, the fountain, which runs up a $250,000-a-year electricity bill to pump 30,000 tons of water through its concrete limbs, has had its fans as well as detractors.

The environment in which it is set has been greatly altered. The work was juxtaposed to the Embarcadero Freeway, which some saw as an appropriate pairing: massive concrete against more massive concrete. When the 1989 Loma Prieta earthquake led to the demise of the freeway, the jagged sculpture remained nestled at the heart of what is becoming one of the great waterfront boulevards of the world.

In 2004, following a three-year drought that had mandated that the Vaillancourt remain waterless, some San Francisco politicians made the suggestion that the fountain be demolished, arguing that the structure was now out of place, expensive to maintain, and an attractive nuisance that acted as a sleeping shelter for the homeless.

Armand Vaillancourt reacted predictably, saying, "They have no right to touch this artwork. I gave almost five years of my life to create that…I'm going to fight like the devil to preserve that work."

As it turned out, city leaders reached a compromise and the fountain's waters now flow—at least periodically—partially supported with private funds.

Who's This?

10. John McLaren

John McLaren, the man here pensively engaged with a pine cone, spent 53 years of his life, until his death in 1943, improving and protecting the 1,000-plus acres that are Golden Gate Park.

This statue fronting the park's grove of rhododendrons, McLaren's favorite flower, was a tribute he had not sought. In fact, after the piece was executed at the insistence of a friend, he hid it under a pile of blankets at the park's stables. The work was only found after his death. In general, statues, or "stookies" as he called them, were not part of his vision for the park. The park's flora was beautiful; stookies, weren't. "Why must people change beautiful things?" he asked. It's appropriate that McLaren's feet are planted firmly on the ground, unlike the park's many other bronze tributes mounted on imposing pedestals. In taking the job of Golden Gate Park Superintendent, he told the city fathers, "There will be no 'Keep off the grass' signs."

Averse to statues as he was, McLaren countered their proliferation with a demonstration of the political savvy that allowed him to survive a long career. He would not squabble over the installation of bronzed war heroes, assassinated presidents, and revered literary lights. He would just plant foliage around them to obscure their impact. Some of the most luxuriant groves in the park are there to obscure a statuary intrusion of which McLaren disapproved.

A gardener since his early teens in Scotland, McLaren was totally into preserving nature in the park. He planted thousands of trees during his tenure while fighting off the encroachment of trolley lines, paving projects, horseless carriages, and later, automobiles into the park. In one instance, a San Francisco police chief wanted to remove an oak tree that he thought was in danger of collapsing onto the Park Police Station. McLaren told the chief he would compromise: "I'll remove the tree if you remove the station."

Something of a dour and hard-headed Scotsman, McLaren was not the easiest person to work for. He said he wouldn't hire anyone who applied wearing a jacket because he suspected that such an applicant would not be up to hard work outdoors. Any employee caught smoking on the job would find himself out of work.

Despite his quirkiness, San Francisco showered their park superintendent with a love highly unusual in a city that enjoys bringing public officials down to earth. Each year his birthday became an excuse for civic celebration. When he reached the mandatory retirement age of 70, the city fathers amended the City Charter to allow him to stay on the job the rest of his life. He took full advantage of this perk. He lived to be 96.

Who's This?

11. Alma Spreckels

Posing at the apex of Union Square's Dewey Monument is Alma Charlotte Corday le Normand de Bretteville—later to become Alma Spreckels, of the sugar baron Spreckels.

Alma started life poor. Her family lived amid the sand dunes of San Francisco's then undeveloped Sunset District, clinging to its aristocratic name and pretensions to highfalutin blood. By 1895, the 14-year-old Alma had left school to work in her family's laundry, picking up dirty clothes from the homes of the city's elite, an experience that whetted her appetite for the good life. Among Alma's assets were a striking beauty and a statuesque 6-foot frame. Her physical attributes, she came to understand, were moneymakers. She began posing as an artist's model, her voluptuous and mostly nude figure coming to adorn the back bar of many a Barbary Coast saloon.

Alma reached the pinnacle (literally and figuratively) of her modeling career when she was hired by sculptor Robert Aitken to model for the Union Square monument he was creating to honor Admiral George Dewey, the hero of the Spanish-American War. In recent years, the square has been redesigned, but "Big Alma," as she came to be known, is still there, her right arm holding the laurel wreath of peace, her left arm raised pointing a trident toward heaven.

About the time she did this modeling, Alma met and was courted by Adolph Spreckels, 22 years her senior. Adolph was the son of Claus Spreckels, who—when he bested the king of Hawaii in a poker game—acquired thousands of acres on Maui that launched his career as the sugar and shipping czar of the west coast.

Adolph was a quiet man of philanthropic inclination, whose career hit a pronounced glitch in 1884 when he shot—but did not quite kill—Michael H. de Young, co-founder of the *San Francisco Chronicle,* who had accused him of defrauding stockholders. The jury, sympathetic to Spreckels temporary insanity plea, acquitted the sugar heir.

Adolph put off marriage to Alma for five years until 1908, perhaps because he was carrying around a case of syphilis that, fortunately for Alma, remained in a latent state during the years of their marriage.

In 1913, Adolph built a "great white wedding cake of a house on Washington Street" for his bride, indulging Alma's every whim. The site itself was

chosen so that the Spreckels would be able to overlook, not only the bay, but the Panama Pacific International Exposition of 1915 underway in the Marina District. In an admirable precursor of the preservationist mentality, Alma had structures on the property moved in order to escape demolition and installed on the brick-paved block of Octavia Street the landscaped islands that are still there today. In keeping with the emerging automobile culture, the property included a vast garage featuring a turntable so that no Rolls-Royce driver would ever need to back in or out.

More recently, the property has been the residence of Danielle Steel, the romance novelist, and her large brood of children. One would expect they had enough space to spread out in the 55 original rooms on the property. Even so, Steel added a few more.

Why Is This There?

12. The Murphy Windmill

The Murphy Windmill—named after Samuel Murphy, the windmill-loving philanthropist who donated $20,000 in 1908 to pay for its construction—is said to be the largest structure of its kind in the world. The Murphy, located at the southwest edge of Golden Gate Park, joined the 1902 Dutch Windmill, a quarter-mile to the north, in performing the vital duty of drawing water from underground springs to green the western end of the park.

This once desolate area needed all the help it could get. In 1867, Mayor Frank McCoppin, recognizing that a growing San Francisco population would need open space for recreation, proposed a park on what was known as the Outside Lands. As this part of town was a howling desert of shifting winds, no real estate interests were competing for the property, so the idea went forward unimpeded.

The challenge was to turn dunes into a park. The city approached Frederick Law Olmsted, the dean of American landscape architects, who, in 1858, had completed New York's Central Park. Olmsted said, "Sorry," thinking it couldn't be done, even wondering if "trees that delight" could be grown in San Francisco.

This negativity did not infect William Hammond Hall, a 25-year-old engineer, hired in 1870 to produce a topographical map of the 1,013 acres that were to become Golden Gate Park. Full of ambition, but with absolutely no knowledge of landscape architecture beyond what he had read in books, he signed on to make a park. Perhaps surprisingly, the area to the east of what is now 14th Avenue proved not much of a problem. Hall discovered dark sandy loam with excellent drainage and underground streams that provided plenty of water. The difficulty was to be with the remaining 730 windswept, treeless and sandy acres sprawling toward Ocean Beach. The plants, which he hoped would take hold, could not survive long enough to put down roots. Then one day, barley from a horse's feeding bag fell in the area. The barley took hold, and when Hall mixed it with lupine and manure he had his recipe to bring bloom to San Francisco's desert. By 1879, Hall had planted 155,000 trees in the park.

But the trees needed water. The monopolistic Spring Valley Water Company was happy to meet the demand at exorbitant rates. When John McLaren, the legendary and long-time park director, took over park duties in 1887, he was shocked by the water bill. He pushed a plan for windmills at Ocean Beach,

which would draw on underground springs near the ocean's edge. That's when Murphy came to the rescue. The windmills churned away just beautifully, pumping as much as 1.5 million gallons a day. In 1913 electric pumps were installed, making the rotating sails irrelevant. As the structures no longer served a practical purpose, they encountered years of neglect. By the 1990s, either the windmills had to be repaired or they had to go. Thus alerted, during the next decade the city and private donors contributed significant money for restoration of these landmarks. They are now looking about as good as they did a century ago, and not a moment too soon. These days, wind power is back.

How Did This Get Built?

13. Neiman Marcus/City of Paris

This harlequin motif wall at the corner of Geary and Stockton Streets is the exterior of the Neiman Marcus building, a structure that bears little resemblance to the great beaux arts edifice that once inhabited this space and was home to the City of Paris, San Francisco's classiest department store.

The origins of the City of Paris go back to 1850, when a French silk-stocking manufacturer, Felix Verdier, showed up in San Francisco Bay with a ship loaded with silks, laces, fine wines, champagne, and cognac. The ship was surrounded by residents in rowboats flush from the gold fields, who bought the contents of the ship before it had a chance to dock. Verdier realized he was on to something and returned a year later with another shipload, staying on to establish the City of Paris Dry Goods Company.

In the 1906 earthquake and fire, the interior of the building that housed the City of Paris was destroyed while the exterior remained intact. This gave renowned San Francisco architect Arthur Brown Jr. a chance to redo the interior with features that included an opulent rotunda with a stained-glass dome.

For more than a century the City of Paris was a special place. Here you could buy kid's books in French and purchase and exchange rare stamps. There was a booth with a woman who cut out and sold black silhouettes. Each holiday season, the rotunda housed the official San Francisco Christmas tree. The Verdier family still owned the store in the 1970s, by which time their charming and elegant way of doing business was no longer in style.

Enter, in 1974, the corporate presence of Neiman Marcus with a interest in buying the building. But the new Texas owners found the space unsuited for modern merchandising and said it had to come down. They hired San Francisco architect John Carl Warneke, whose design was so unfortunate in the eyes of his 24-year-old daughter that she pleaded with city officials to stop her father from building it. The project stalled, and it wasn't until 1979 that famous architect Phillip Johnson was given the green light to go ahead with the existing building after he came up with a plan to preserve the City of Paris rotunda and dome.

Still, many citizens were unhappy to lose the City of Paris building. Some 55,000 signatures opposing the destruction of the revered building were collected; 20 organizations rallied in support. The City of Paris was listed in the

Rotunda of the City of Paris

National Register of Historic Places, but in 1981 the structure came down. Johnson explained how he hoped the public would come to appreciate the new building. He told the *San Francisco Examiner* that the wall pattern "comes from a Renaissance palace I saw in Perugia." On another occasion he said, the building's facade should be viewed as an abstract painting, "like a Mondrian."

At least one planning commissioner didn't see it that way. The building was about as exciting, he said, as "the PG&E substation at Larkin and Eddy."

The controversy over the City of Paris building had its upside. Charles Hall Page, founder of San Francisco Heritage said that until the City of Paris uproar, "[Preservationists] focused on Victorian houses. People thought they were neat and cute and should be protected. People were unaware that we had some fine commercial buildings downtown." Now that's changed. Historical downtown buildings have organizations and advocates on their side, who stand ready to—when necessary—fend off the wrecking ball.

Why Is This There?

14. Japanese Tea Garden

The Moon Bridge at Golden Gate Park's Japanese Tea Garden is intended to provide the visitor with a tranquil experience, as one stands at the apex observing one's image reflected in the water below. In 1894, however, when the California Midwinter International Exposition brought a Japanese village to the park, tranquility did not seem to be an exposition priority.

The peaceful Japanese simulation was one exception to the otherwise visual cacophony of exhibits, 100 buildings on 200 acres that transported the world in all its dissonance to San Francisco. There was a Forty-Niner camp, an Eskimo village—featuring dog teams and papier-mâché igloos—various Native American tribal camps, a Chinese gambling house, South Sea Islanders, and a Cairo street scene featuring camels and whirling dervishes. There was room for a Hindu temple that served as the exposition's administration building as well as Moorish rotundas and Oriental minarets. However, superficial and stereotypical these displays may have been, The *Overland Monthly* made the point that the exposition, "affords peeps into lands and customs that have hitherto been myth, as far away and implacable as the-man-in-the-moon."

The mover behind the exposition was Michael de Young, publisher of the *San Francisco Chronicle.* De Young noted that the Chicago World's Fair of 1893 had been a huge pick-me-up for that city, which, like the rest of the country, had been mired in depression. Why not, he reasoned, bring a similar exposition to San Francisco? But de Young would do Chicago one better. This would be the *Midwinter* Exposition, demonstrating to the world that, in California, February temperatures are no reason to stay indoors. On January 27, 1894, the festivities opened. This fast track had been possible because, with the Chicago event shutting down, many of the fair's exhibits were eager to relocate to San Francisco. The directors siphoned off the best of these.

The centerpiece at the exposition was the 266-foot-high Bonet's Tower. (Leopold Bonet, its designer, had been one of the architects of the Chicago event.) The structure was considered a little sister to the Eiffel Tower, which had been completed in 1889. In keeping with the electricity craze of the day, the tower was all about light; 3,200 multicolored incandescent lights were topped by the world's most powerful searchlight that its promoters claimed emitted a light so strong that one could read a newspaper under its rays 10 miles away.

All of the buildings, with the exception of what was to be the de Young Museum, were temporary. (The copper, stone, and glass de Young of today is its third iteration.) No one was more eager to begin destruction when the exposition closed than John McLaren, the park superintendent, who had lost this particular battle in his continuing war to keep the park green. When the owners of the electric tower dragged their feet in removing it, McLaren wasted no time in dynamiting it.

McLaren made one exception to his demolition derby. When Makoto Hagiwara, a wealthy local Japanese landscape designer, appealed to him to allow him to convert the Japanese village into the Japanese Tea Garden, McLaren recognized that a refuge filled with flowering cherry trees, oriental magnolias, and dwarf pines would fit right into his master plan. Today, despite a bumpy ride that included sending the Hagiwaras off to an internment camp in 1942, the Japanese Tea Garden, early on a weekday morning, remains the tranquil sea it had been in the midst of frenetic activity more than 100 years ago.

Why Is This There?

15. The Palace of Fine Arts

By all rights, the Palace of Fine Arts, the building that its renowned architect Bernard Maybeck called his "'dream of the past," should have joined the junk heap of history, along with the other extravagant structures created for the 1915 Panama Pacific International Exposition. The whole grandiose mélange, built mostly of plaster, burlap, and chicken wire, was meant to destruct when the exposition ended. The palace was to be no exception.

But that demise has been put off by fits and starts. Concerned citizens led by Phoebe Apperson Hearst, mother of the newspaper mogul, raised funds to save the palace from the wrecking ball when the exposition closed in December 1915. This effort did not spare the building from the ravages of age and neglect. By World War II, vehicles from the Presidio Motor Pool had taken up residence at the once verdant palace grounds. By the mid-1960s, with the structure on its last legs, the state of California and philanthropist-hero Walter Johnson stepped in to fund its rebuilding in reinforced concrete. But the building kept demanding more. Over the next decades mold, bacteria, rust, animal

The Palace of Fine Arts in 1915.

deposits, and the Loma Prieta earthquake sent the building on a downward spiral. Once more, lovers of the property came through with money to make repairs. In 2011, the building was spruced up and reinforced to the max, our own little Parthenon.

The story of how the palace got here in the first place is one worth telling. In 1904, San Franciscans eagerly awaited the finishing touches on the Panama Canal, a development that would cut 8,000 miles off the sea route to California and was expected to bring an economic boom not seen since the Gold Rush. There was talk of an exposition to celebrate the canal's completion. Alas, the earthquake and fire of 1906 put these big ideas on hold. By 1908 the city was well on the way to rebuilding. Exposition plans were now revived, this time not only to celebrate the canal, but also to announce to the world that San Francisco was back, better than ever. A swampland site known as Washerwoman's Cove, running from Van Ness Avenue to Fort Point, was identified, and 635 acres of it, using largely the ruins of 1906, were filled. So in 1915, what is now the Marina District became a fantasy land of gardens, sculptures, towers, palaces, obelisks, courts, and fountains. There was a 65-acre amusement park, 1,500 pieces of sculpture, a working replica of the Panama Canal, and the 435-foot Tower of Jewels with 135,000 specially cut glass prisms.

As the early years of the 20th century were full of entrepreneurial and technological breakthroughs, the exposition was able to spotlight the latest sewing machines and typewriters, indirect lighting and the long-distance telephone. Henry Ford put up a production line that produced more than 3,000 automobiles during the festivities.

During its 288-day existence, the exposition drew 18 million visitors, 20 times the population of San Francisco. By the end of the event, Maybeck was ready to say goodbye to his building. "I should like, that my palace dies of its own accord, and becomes its own cemetery," he said. By 1957, just before his death at 95, he had changed his mind. Then he saw the palace as "probably the last of the traditional pieces of architecture to survive in the modem age." Let's remember that.

What Happened Here?

16. Room 1221—St. Francis Hotel

n 1921, behind a door of the St. Francis Hotel transpired a piece of celebrity sleaze worthy of our own time. The hotel has always accommodated the whims of famous guests. The concierge indulged Richard Nixon's late night Oreo cravings and provided the actress wife of impresario Florenz Ziegfield with 30 gallons of milk each day for her lactose bath. Playing host to the rich and famous can have a downside, however, as was evident on September 4, 1921 when silent screen comedian Roscoe "Fatty" Arbuckle and some friends came up from Hollywood and checked into rooms 1218-1221 to get a party going.

Unfortunately for Arbuckle, the wrong party crashers showed up. One was Maude Delmont, an amateur blackmailer, and the other was Virginia Rappe, a "starlet" known to most everyone at Arbuckle's Keystone Studios for her willingness to provide generous and up-close services to the studio's male employees. Rappe was also known as a blackout drinker who could not hold her liquor. In room 1221 she was putting this reputation to the test, guzzling uncontrollably, and ripping off her clothes. When she passed out, Arbuckle moved her to one of the other rooms to sleep it off. The next day he returned to Southern California, where he got the word: Virginia Rappe was dead and Maude Delmont was fingering him as Rappe's assailant and rapist.

The Hearst press raised the stakes claiming, with no evidence whatever, that Arbuckle had penetrated Rappe using a Coke bottle. Meanwhile, the papers restored Rappe's pre-Coke bottle virginity. Some 8,000 strangers attended her funeral at St. Stephens Episcopal Church in East Hollywood.

After Arbuckle was arrested, the San Francisco D. A., one Matthew Brady, a man who wanted to be governor of California, pursued the case with a vengeance. He thought a victory in the Arbuckle case would send him on his way to Sacramento. So Arbuckle was tried three times. Two trials ended in hung juries. In the third trial, when the defense was allowed to make its complete case, including evidence about the machinations of Maude Delmont, the jury deliberated only six minutes before acquittal.

Arbuckle's victory was a hollow one. The movie moguls, taking the heat for the public perception of the film colony as a hot bed of immorality, made an example of Arbuckle, deciding he would never work in their town again. In 1933, at age 46, Arbuckle died—broke. Those closest to him said it was a broken heart that did him in.

What Happened Here?

17. Balmy Alley

I n the 1970s, here on Balmy Alley, off of 24th Street near Harrison, the seeds of an artistic revolution were planted when Patricia Rodriguez, a Latina resident and artist, decided it would be an exhilarating visual upgrade to supplement the exterior of her residence with a mural. When she approached her neighbors to determine if they, too, would like to beautify their little street of garage doors and back fences, she was not greeted with much enthusiasm. She was able to enlist a couple of recruits though and that was enough to touch off the most prolific and diverse collection of neighborhood street art in the United States.

As it happened, this modest beginning coincided with a decade when the Mission District was exploding intellectually and artistically. Neighborhood residents, some 65 percent Latino, were becoming alert to the Central American revolutions against oppressive and undemocratic regimes, particularly in El Salvador and Nicaragua. Representatives of the Chicano movement became articulate voices in the neighborhood, and the young Latino—mostly male— artists now saw murals as a tool for making political statements. This dedication, coupled with the introduction of acrylic paint that made it possible for outdoor art to withstand the elements, filled neighborhood walls with politically-based art.

In Balmy Alley, art went up depicting the struggle of Latin American peasants for land and dignity. Other Mission murals were history-based, portraying the indigenous people of the Americas confronting the swords of conquistadors.

Rodriguez and her female colleagues, who became collectively known as the *Mujeres Muralistas,* wanted to supplement these aggressive political depictions. Their murals portrayed a rich Latino culture focusing on community, family, and children. Their world was often one of festivals, harvests, and flowers. A typically positive mural on Folsom Street shows United Farm Workers founder Cesar Chavez leading a group of children through the California fields.

Artists of both sexes began to focus on the mythic traditions of Latino culture. A mural in a minipark near 24th and Bryant Streets tells the story of the Aztec deity Quetzalcoatl, the feathered serpent. The myth of the creation of the Mexican volcanoes Popocatepetl and Iztaccihuatl is related on the wall of a bakery at Alabama and 24th Streets.

In recent years the murals here have become more eclectic both in style and content. One of the first Balmy Alley murals was created by schoolchildren and that tradition continues, often under the supervision of the Mission-based arts group Precita Eyes, which over its 35-year existence has been responsible for 500 murals in San Francisco. Some contemporary artists now work with spray paint and create cartoonish and pop art images. Politics is still present, but is more likely to be taking on neighborhood gentrification than American imperialism.

detail of "Victorion: El Defensor de la Misión" mural in Balmy Alley by Sirron Norris.

Now, going on 50 years since the first murals were birthed on Balmy Alley and nearby Streets, murals brighten nearly every San Francisco neighborhood. Yet nowhere are they more of a delightful and essential part of the community than in the Mission District.

First Balmy Alley mural painted by Patricia Rodriguez and the *Mujeres Muralistas*.

Why Is This There?

18. The Old Ship Saloon

The model sailing ship that welcomes imbibers to the Old Ship Saloon at the corner of Battery Street and Pacific Avenue provides a reminder of what lies beneath: an old ship. How a ship found its way to this inland corner takes some explaining. In 1849, at the peak of the California Gold Rush, the three-masted vessel *Arkansas* collided with rocks off Alcatraz Island. Here it remained until an enterprising Englishman named Joe Anthony hauled it to its current location and in 1851 opened the Old Ship Ale House. Ferrying the ship to this destination was no great feat as what is now the intersection of Battery and Pacific was then part of San Francisco Bay. A gang plank connected the ship-saloon to the Pacific Pier.

Meanwhile, other go-getters were engaged in landfill operations that effectively landlocked the *Arkansas*. So in 1859, the above-ground section of the ship was demolished and replaced by the existing structure. It was then that the saloon became notorious as a hotbed of Shanghaiing—the practice of waylaying seamen for voyages to points unknown that was standard operating procedure in this neighborhood known as the Barbary Coast.

Shanghaiing caught sailors in a revolving aquatic door. Here's how it worked. When a ship arrived in port it would be deluged by "runners" employed by boarding house owners of the neighborhood. They were charged with inducing crew members back to their employers' establishments. A runner would bring with him the tools of his trade: brass knuckles, large quantities of liquor, obscene photos, and, in some cases, liquid soap. His job was to get the sailor drunk, then show him the dirty pictures as a way of inviting him to shoreline pleasures. If that didn't work, the brass knuckles provided a further inducement. Finally, a bowl of galley soup spiked with the soap could be the ultimate convincer. Many ship captains did not discourage these shenanigans because a man who "deserted" the ship did not have to be paid.

Once ashore the seaman's unfortunate journey had just begun. Ensconced at the proprietor's lodging, he was offered generous portions of Ludlum-dosed whiskey, a concoction that soon left him sleeping like a baby. Conveyed to the basement of the establishment, often via a trap door in the saloon's floor, the comatose man would be sacked up and delivered to a departing vessel in need of a crew. Greed-inspired creativity being what it is, however, these rascals did not transport only the living. In some cases corpses and straw dummies were

also foisted on crew-needy captains. The verisimilitude of these phony packages was often increased by sewing a twitching rat to its contents to provide a sign of life.

The Old Ship was far from the only saloon specializing in Shanghaiing. The most famous Shanghaier of all, Shanghai Kelly, operated out of a nearby establishment at 33 Pacific, now a neatly manicured office and condo complex.

By the beginning of the 20th century, the practice of Shanghaiing was dying out, suppressed through federal legislation, the rise of the seafarers unions, and the decline of sail-propelled ships, which had depended on seamen more valued for their brawn than for their brains.

What's This?

19. Earthquake Cottages

There were once more than 5,000 of these structures in San Francisco. Now at least 20 remain, but there may be many more. Built in response to the San Francisco earthquake and fire of 1906 that destroyed 28,000 buildings and left about a quarter million people homeless, these cottages, resembling nothing so much as the little tokens on a Monopoly board, were the FEMA trailers of their day.

After the earthquake and fire, thousands fled to the city's parks where they were temporarily housed in tents. For the most part, these were poor people: the seamstresses, maids, bricklayers, and metal workers who had resided in tenements demolished by the earthquake or destroyed in the conflagration—people who had never owned property. A particularly rainy spring and summer made life in the tents more than uncomfortable and prompted the city to action.

Between September 1906 and March 1907, San Francisco recruited union carpenters to construct thousands of cottages, many of which were as small as 10 feet by 14 feet. They were equipped with stoves, but had no plumbing. Baths and toilets were communal. The cottages were all painted green to harmonize with the park settings. Photographs of the time show hundreds of these structures placed cheek by jowl in Mission (Dolores) Park, Washington Square, and other open spaces.

Eugene Schmitz, then mayor of the city, was beginning to worry that the residents of these structures would never want to leave their new homes. Indeed, health department officials reported that the cottage dwellers were flourishing as they had not in the slum conditions in which they previously resided. The city came up with a plan. Relief officials had been collecting $2 a month rent from the cottage dwellers. Now they refunded the rent and handed over the cottages to their occupants free and clear on the condition that they would haul the structures out of the parks. A new homeowner could use his rebate toward the purchase of land on which to place his new acquisition. Many of the cottages found their way to the western and southern areas of the city where the land was cheap.

Today, it's not always easy to identify an earthquake cottage. Many have been demolished, of course, but others have been renovated beyond recognition. The cottage pictured here has been moved to the Presidio from its previous Richmond District location.

Why Does This Look Familiar?

20. V. C. Morris Building—
140 Maiden Lane

The V. C. Morris Building on Maiden Lane is New York's Guggenheim Museum in miniature. You'll need to pass through the arched doorway to get the full effect, but once you've entered this space—the only Frank Lloyd Wright building within the city limits of San Francisco—the parallels are unmistakable. The curving ramp and the skylights look like a warm-up for the New York structure.

Whether Wright was using this jewel of a building as a tryout for the larger structure is a matter of debate. Designed specifically as a high-end gift store for the V. C. Morrises, the plans for the building were competed in 1948 when Wright was 81, that's about the time he was working on the design for the Guggenheim. The Morris Building, constructed within the envelope of an existing site, took much prep work and wasn't up and running until 1953. The Morrises invested so heavily in the building that they were unable to go ahead with construction of the Sea Cliff home that Wright had also designed for them.

The museum, of course a much more ambitious project, was completed in 1957. As gift stores go, the Morris Building's exterior may be unique. Wright wanted no "vulgarizing display of merchandise" luring customers from behind street-level windows. Instead, he believed the building itself to be its advertisement.

The result, wrote *Chronicle* architecture critic Alan Temko, was, "a reticent façade that is, by any standards, one of the great walls of the world, minimalist art that isn't minimalist."

What Happened To …?

21. Classic Ferries

Yes, beautiful vessels like the ferryboat *Eureka*, now berthed at the Hyde Street Pier at Aquatic Park, are gone, but today we have fast and efficient ships—moving up to 40 miles per hour—connecting the San Francisco waterfront with Larkspur, Vallejo, Sausalito, Alameda and other destinations.

Today's ferries are not the large and stately vessels that, up until the mid-1930s, dotted the bay. The completion of the bay-spanning bridges, the San Francisco-Oakland Bay Bridge in 1936 and the Golden Gate Bridge in 1937, spelled almost instant obsolescence for these majestic boats. Vessels like the *Eureka*, launched in 1890 as the *Ukiah*, offered commuters a water adventure in an elegant setting of polished brass and wood paneling.

It was the Southern Pacific Railroad that saw the necessity to create a ferry fleet. Without the ferries, transcontinental railroad passengers would be stranded in Oakland, the railway terminus. The S. P. ferries became the "tracks across the bay." From the 1920s until 1936, these vessels carried 50,000 passengers a year.

As with today's ferries, business deals and first dates could be part of the mix, but because the ships were slower (it took a ferry one hour and 30 minutes to make the journey from San Francisco to Vallejo), food was also a big deal. During the Great Depression years, a commuter on the *Eureka* could enjoy Kidney Sauté on Toast or Boiled Beef Brisket with Spanish Sauce, each for 40 cents, accompanied, perhaps, by an Acme beer or a Rainer Ale for an additional 20 cents. Even on the shorter runs food was front and center. Ferry historian Harry Demoro recalled that on the 18-minute trip from Oakland to the Ferry Building the boats had 12-slice automatic electric toasters to speed up breakfast preparation.

Riders came to cherish tangential aspects of their commute. Maybe they would spot Peg-Legged Pete, the one-legged seagull, or make the cross-bay journey on the vessel tended by "The Caruso of the Ferries," the boatman who sang opera arias to his delighted captive audience.

Along with the decline of the ferries came the dismemberment of Arthur Brown Jr.'s 1898 Ferry Building. In 1955, the mosaic floor and dramatic brick and ceramic arches of the building's sun-filled great hall were hidden behind sheet rock as the space was parceled into offices. A couple of years later, the

building was further assaulted by the intrusion of the double-deck Embarcadero Freeway, built across its face. The freeway remained for 35 years.

But by the 1970s, the ferry system and—two decades later—the Ferry
Building began to breathe new life. Traffic congestion on the bridges was not
pretty, and the new ferries and the BART system stepped into the breach.
Now there are about 130 ferry arrivals and departures from the Ferry Building
each day, about half what it was in the 1930s, but still a healthy number.

But it's not like it once was. In 1964, Herb Caen rued the difference: "Today thousands of people live at the edge of the bay they've never been on. A
bridge is only a highway in the sky. Ferryboats were close to the foaming heart
of the matter—something to love."

What's This?

22. Columbus Tower

Today this building at 916 Kearny Street is the center for enterprises engaged in by its owner, film director Francis Ford Coppola. While movie buffs may pay homage at the location where *The Godfather* was edited, students of bad government should also pay heed. This was the building where San Francisco's most notorious political boss, Abe Ruef, tried to do business during his final years.

Ruef developed this structure, then known as the Sentinel Building, in 1906 at the height of his political power. With the building nearing completion, all but its steel skeleton was destroyed in the 1906 earthquake and fire. It was soon reconstructed, but for five years Ruef was unable to use it as his headquarters, the reason being he was an inmate at San Quentin.

How Abe Ruef ended up in prison is a story worth telling. Ruef was not exactly your up-from-the-Streets Tammany Hall-type boss. A native San Franciscan from a prominent Jewish family, he graduated from the University of California at age 18 able to speak eight languages—including Cantonese—and was admitted to the California Bar at 21. Initially drawn to reform politics, and corresponding with the likes of Theodore Roosevelt, the undertow of political corruption proved too tempting for his ambitious instincts.

Neither the Democrats nor Republicans had much use for Ruef, nor he for them. Recognizing that working people in San Francisco had nowhere to turn to in a political system in which political parties kowtowed to the Southern Pacific Railroad and used police to protect strikebreakers, Ruef decided to organize another party, the aptly named Union Labor Party, given his target voter. As Ruef considered the strictures of public office rather too confining, and with a mayoral election coming up, the boss needed a malleable candidate who would do his bidding. He found his perfect empty vessel in Eugene Schmitz, a violinist and the president of the local musicians union. Schooling Schmitz in the art of California politics, Ruef had his prodigy memorize the state Constitution and the City Charter. Schmitz was able to smoothly deliver the speeches that Ruef wrote for him. Surprising everybody but Ruef, Schmitz won. Within a couple of years, members of the Union Labor Party, made up almost entirely of semiliterate and inexperienced pols eager to partake in the spoils of government, dominated the Board of Supervisors.

Ruef set up a system that looked out for his colleagues, but mostly for

Ruef. If the telephone company or the electric company wanted a particular piece of legislation passed or stopped, they would hire the legal consultancy services of Abe Ruef for a retainer starting at $10,000 or so. He would take his 50 percent cut and pass on the remainder to Schmitz and the supervisors to be divided up. This worked well enough before the scandal of the "French restaurants." The restaurants might be serving *coq au vin* on the ground floor, but the upper floors were sexual playgrounds for the rich. With the prodding of maverick District Attorney William Langdon, the city embarked on one of its periodic morality binges and the French restaurants, sure enough "clients" of Abe Ruef, were caught in the crossfire. Running scared, some of Ruef's colleagues turned on him, leading to his arrest. After a painfully long trial, characterized by enough defense dodges to provide any loophole-conscious lawyer with textbook lessons, Ruef was convicted and sentenced

to 14 years in prison of which he served five. On his release, he set up offices on the top floors of the Sentinel Building, where he must have enjoyed the view, but did little business. He died penniless in 1936.

Ruef getting advice from attorney Henry Achs outside courthouse, 1907.

Who Thought of This?

23. Bay to Breakers

In 1912, the city was in need of a bit of public relations to show the world the town was back from the horrific earthquake and fire of 1906 that left 250,000 people homeless in a city of about 400,000. The city fathers thought a well-publicized foot race would do the trick, one they called the Cross City Race. The race is still around but it's now dubbed Bay to Breakers. Perhaps coincidentally, the course for the first event coincided with the route earthquake and fire refugees had trekked as they walked up Hayes Street to Alamo Square (just before the race's 3-mile marker) to the central first-aid station and on to what was the location of the tent cities in Golden Gate Park. That's still the route of today's race.

For many years, participation in the event remained low and low key. Until the early 1960s there were no more than 130 men—supplemented by a few disguised women, who had managed to infiltrate this guys-only ritual. (In 1971, the race was opened to all.)

In 1964, someone with an ear for alliteration renamed the Cross City Race the Bay to Breakers and the festivities began to loosen up considerably. Folks began to slow down and costume up. Here's a small portion of what one observer reported seeing in 1982: a guy dressed as a dog dish; another decked out as a San Francisco fern bar complete with empty glasses, crumpled name tags, and used ashtrays; a man in pajamas and a woman in a baby-doll nightgown with a sign on her back reading, "I got up late;" another woman in a t-shirt that read, "I'd rather be having multiple orgasms." And that was in the days when things were relatively sane.

Do not, however, think this what-the-hell playfulness of many has made the race less serious for others. In addition to real runners from all around the world, the race also features the celebrated centipede teams—competing groups of a minimum of 13 runners tethered together. They may be costumed as a string of DNA molecules or a linear accelerator, but they can be dead on serious, often practicing for months before the competition.

Like other San Francisco events, Bay to Breakers has its subcultures of participants. One which needs no explanation is the group Bare to Breakers. The group's motivating mantra might serve as watchword for many race participants: "There is a time when people reach a point in their lives when they just say, 'Why not?'"

What's This?

24. Cameron House

This substantial building at 920 Sacramento Street, known as the Donaldina Cameron House, ranks high among San Francisco's allegedly haunted locations. While ghostbusters can produce an impressive list of other frequently seen apparitions—for instance, the woman in white at Stow Lake, said to be searching for her toddler who drowned in a boating accident; and the appearance in the lobby mirror of the Curran Theater of the ghostly image of a ticket taker, murdered there in the 1930s—none of these sightings compare in poignancy and cultural significance with the demise of the young Chinese women whose eerie personages are said to revisit the building after being burned to death here behind a locked door.

Here's how this tragedy happened. Donaldina Cameron, a 19-year-old New Zealander, arrived at this address in 1888, then the Presbyterian Mission House, to teach sewing to residents of the mission, all young Chinese girls. The Mission House had not been these girls' first stop in the United States. Most of them had been shipped from China at a prepubescent age to work as indentured servants in San Francisco. Others had been kidnapped and sold as household slaves. In both cases, when the girls reached womanhood, their lives entered a new chapter. They were sold into short, violent, and miserable lives as prostitutes, a "career" that offered a life expectancy of about five years.

The Presbyterian mission was committed to rescuing these young women, but with the arrival of Donaldina Cameron the organization's commitment became a fervent cause. Cameron had an uncanny knack of smelling out the brothels, often hidden behind trap doors. Sometimes enlisting the help of the Chinatown police squad, she would be engaged in action-movie type chases over rooftops and down dark alleys. To the tongs, the criminal organizations that bankrolled the brothels, Cameron was *Fahn Quai*, the white devil, and "the Jesus woman," who, they told their captives, would drink the blood of the liberated girls to keep up her vitality.

Cameron, while not a blood drinker, did indeed have an agenda: to convert her emancipated charges to Christianity. She rescued and educated an estimated 3,000 girls. While many took positively to the transformation, calling Cameron *Lo Ma*, (little mother) and even naming their children "Donaldina," others ran away from the home.

The Mission House was regularly under assault, sometimes by the brothel

owners, but also, ironically, by the police sent by the powers-that-be to roust "illegal aliens." So in 1908, after the mission was demolished in the 1906 earthquake and fire, Cameron made sure the basement of the new structure was constructed with hidden passages behind which the girls could hide. Some years later, when a fire broke out, several of the girls were trapped and burned to death in the very rooms that were supposed to keep them safe. It is these unfortunate souls that are believed to have been left behind to haunt the premises.

While today Cameron House acts as a neighborhood social service center, the doors to the basement remain sealed. Knowledge of this disaster has pretty much passed into history except for an occasional sighting of a wispy figure who appears, to believers in such things, to be reminding us of the tragic end of these ill-starred young women.

What's This?

25. Burritt Alley

One searches the annals of San Francisco crime in vain for mention of the nefarious deed described on this plaque placed on the wall at Burritt Alley and Bush Street. That's because the event occurred only in the imagination of Dashiell Hammett, author of the noir novel based in San Francisco, *The Maltese Falcon*.

See, near the beginning of the novel, Brigid O'Shaughnessy, who we learn later is posing as a Miss Wonderly, hires Miles Archer to scare Floyd Thursby, who she wants to get out of the way so he won't interfere with her plans to get her hands on the jewel-encrusted Maltese Falcon. But Thursby doesn't scare, so she kills Archer to pin the crime on Thursby which . . . then it starts to get complicated.

In addition to commemorating this pivotal event in this most San Francisco of novels, the alley site holds particular significance for Hammett fans because across Bush, a few steps to the northeast from the alley, is Dashiell Hammett Street where, in 1926, Hammett lived at No. 20. It wasn't, of course, Dashiell Hammett Street then, it was Monroe Street. The commemorative renaming is the result of a 1988 campaign by poet and City Lights Book Shop owner Lawrence Ferlinghetti to rename some San Francisco Streets after contributors to San Francisco's literary reputation.

When Hammett lived at 20 Monroe he was not entirely engaged in writing thrillers. He was nursing his recurring tuberculosis and writing advertising copy for Samuels Jewelers at 895 Market. The walk to work would take him daily past Burritt Alley.

In 1927, when he moved to an apartment at 891 Post Street, and got serious about writing *The Maltese Falcon,* he had Burritt Alley as well as the mean Streets of Eddy, Turk, Hyde, Post, and Geary well in mind.

Hammett had arrived in the city in 1921 to continue his work as a Pinkerton detective, an occupation that proved invaluable as he became a weaver of crime stories. He left Pinkerton a year later when the tailing the job required grew too arduous for a man with TB. Making the decision to become a writer, he enrolled in the Munson Secretarial School on Sutter Street long enough to learn typing and began to churn out well-received detective thrillers for *Black Mask* magazine and other "pulps." His base pay of one cent a word rose to six cents a word as readers sought out his stories. All but two of his more than 100 short stories were written while he was in San Francisco. The city's environment in those years, with its speakeasies, tong wars, rum running, and on-the-take politicians could not have been better suited to the fictional milieu Hammitt sought to create.

But, in 1929, Hammett left town before his fame kicked in. He had borrowed $500 from his former employer, Albert Samuels, to kickstart his career in New York and Hollywood. He did, in fact, hit it big with the publication of *The Maltese Falcon*. Returning to the city in a limo, he paid back Samuels, rented a suite at the Fairmont, bought numerous rounds for the denizens of his former hangouts, and, according to Samuels, borrowed another $800 to get out of town. He never came back.

What Happened Here?

26. The Grand Staircase at City Hall

This most elegant of San Francisco staircases, central to the rotunda at San Francisco City Hall, now invites quiet contemplation. Such was not the case on May 13, 1960, when the stairs were awash with sprawling young bodies.

The occasion was a hearing called by a subcommittee of the House Un-American Activities Committee (HUAC). The committee had been set up in 1938 presumably to keep an eye on the activities of Nazis operating in the United States. More than 20 years later, the committee was still in existence, now attempting to smoke out leftist radicals. The congressmen had arrived in San Francisco to expose the "subversive" activities of local Communists although, as one observer commented, "At the time, the Communist Party was too weak to subvert a garden club." That did not stop Edwin Willis, the "Dixicrat" chairman of the committee, from trying to make political hay with his southern constituents.

The hearings in the San Francisco Board of Supervisors chambers were set for three days and were supposed to be open to the public. Among those who wanted to attend were students from local universities, who were emerging from the 1950s stereotype that branded them "The Silent Generation." Their efforts to be admitted, however, were stymied by the "white card" system of preferential seating that stacked the audience with observers favorable to the committee. "We wanted decent people in here," said William Wheeler, liaison to the committee.

By the second day of the hearings, a group of 200 protesters, mostly students, some bearing placards with statements such as "Witch Hunters Go Home," congregated outside the chamber doors demanding first come, first serve admission. What happened next was in dispute. The protestors were making a lot of noise. The officer in charge of the police contingent of 400 cops may have unfurled a fire hose and asked, "You want some of this?" One of the demonstrators may have said, "Go ahead." And that's just what the police did. They later claimed that the demonstrators had surged toward the chamber door before the hoses were set off and that one of the demonstrators had attacked an officer. Photos and footage of the hosing, however, show the kids sitting on the stairs.

In the end, 64 were arrested (the charges against all but one dismissed), and 12 were hospitalized, including eight officers mostly suffering from exhaustion.

The City Hall combat had implications far beyond its immediate casualties. It is said to be the event that, for white youth, touched off the 1960s. Not understanding the tinder box they were about to ignite, HUAC produced a film, *Operation Abolition*, that, using footage of the disturbance, attempted to expose the students as Communist "dupes." However, when the film was shown on college campuses, all the young viewers saw were kids being washed down marble steps by police-manned fire hoses. Many young people arrived in the Bay Area in time to get in on the next big encounter four years later in 1964: The Free Speech Movement at the University of California Berkeley.

A little poem written by one of the City Hall demonstrators capsulated the evolving scene:

> *Silly cops*
>
> *Hosing the crops.*
>
> *Don't they know,*
>
> *They'll make them grow.*

Why Is It Called . . .?

27. Telegraph Hill

Before it became Telegraph Hill this promontory at the northeast corner of the city had several other names. Initially the arriving Spaniards named it *Loma Alta*, "High Hill," a seemingly undeserved designation as, at 295 feet, Telegraph Hill is by no means the highest of the more than 40 San Francisco peaks. (Mount Davidson measures out at 925 feet.) After the Spanish and before 1850, the hill acquired other names, two of which, Goat Hill and Tin Can Hill, provide a clue to the animal population and general tidiness of the location.

With the discovery of gold in the Sierra in 1848, little ethnic clusters of immigrants—famished Irishmen, Chilean miners, discards from Australian prisons—came to live on the hill, mostly in tents. With ships now entering the bay every day, the hill took on new prominence. A young entrepreneur, John K. Duer, saw his main chance. Residents were hungry to get a leg up on news of arriving vessels. On the one hand, the sharpie investors wanted to know what was being delivered so they would not pay too much in a wildly speculative market. On the other hand, everyone else wanted to know right off when the occasional mail packet boat arrived, delivering as many as 13,000 pieces of mail.

Duer's contribution was to erect a little shack topped with a semaphore-like device (like the railroad-crossing semaphores of a later time) at the top of the hill that could be used to signal the city as to the nature of ships entering the bay. The two arms of the device were raised in varied combinations to alert locals to the arrival of, say, a schooner or a sloop of war. A kind of cheat sheet to the symbols was peddled on the streets of the city, but it wasn't long before most residents had committed the signs to memory.

The story goes that when, at a dramatic production, an actor spread his arms wide and proclaimed, "My Lord, what does this mean?" a patron in the audience was fast to respond," Sidewheel steamer." The house roared as everyone got the joke.

Soon, the manually operated device at the top of the hill began to be known as a telegraph. On September 17, 1850, the *Alta California* newspaper made a reference to "Telegraph Hill." The name stuck, even though the telegraph gizmo did not. By 1852, the semaphore had new owners, and the pressure was on for faster information. They responded by building another station several miles away at Point Lobos that would relay information to Telegraph Hill. By mid-1853 the time had arrived for a real telegraph, an electric system that transmitted Morse code signals from Point Lobos to subscribers in the city. After that, no one much looked to the crest of Telegraph Hill to get their messages. The manual telegraph system had lasted only three and a half years, but the little mountain that is its namesake remains known throughout the world.

Inner Telegraph Station.

What's This?

28. The Pioneer Monument

This is the Pioneer Monument, now located at a public space between the Asian Art Museum and the Main Library. Since 1894, the 820-ton piece, by then prominent San Francisco sculptor Frank Happersberger, was a feature of the former Marshall Square, at what is now the intersection of Hyde, Grove, and Market Streets. There it served as a frontice piece for the old Paris-inspired City Hall, a disaster of a building begun in 1870, but plagued by shoddy construction and corrupt contracts. Finally completed in 1897, the building met its predictable demise with the earthquake and fire of 1906. But the sturdy monument remained in place until 1993 when it was moved to its current location to make room for the new library.

The piece was a posthumous gift to the city from pioneer investor, philanthropist and crank James Lick, who had died in 1876. He had designated $100,000 for a monument celebrating the early history of California. Happersberger did not disappoint, cramming a heavy dose of the state's past into this cast iron rendering. Atop the monument is the Roman Goddess Minerva standing in allegorically for *Eureka*, the state's motto (if that makes sense). Artfully posed beneath and near the goddess are two other draped goddesses representing agriculture and commerce, a Mexican *vaquero*, a Franciscan *padre*, a submissive Indian, and a trio of prospectors. A series of bas-reliefs depict more vaqueros, "Trappers Trading Skins With the Indians," and "California's Progress Under American Rule." The names and portraits of all sort of folks prominent in the development of California are also on display. Among those celebrated are Vallejo, Sutter, Stockton, Cabrillo, and—no surprise—James Lick.

Lick was a bit of a case. An accomplished and prosperous builder of pianos, he was 50 years old in 1848 when he arrived in San Francisco, 17 days before the discovery of gold. Buying up large hunks of land, he became very wealthy almost instantly. He was a loner, a gaunt man, who walked up and down Market Street in a dirty black suit. He often spent his evenings slinking through the city's back alleys begging restaurants for bones he claimed he needed for fertilizing his fruit orchards in the South Bay.

Despite his oddball behavior, Lick has left a mark on the Bay Area. In addition to the Pioneer Monument there is the Lick Observatory in Santa Clara County, and in San Francisco: Lick-Wilmerding High School, James Lick Middle School, and, rather incongruously, the James Lick Freeway.

Problems for the Pioneer Monument, however, emerged in 1991 when the city decided it needed to be moved to make room for the new library. Indian groups for a long time had had a problem with the rendering of an Indian posed submissively at the feet of an aggressive vaquero while a Catholic father points dramatically toward heaven. These organizations thought it was time to junk the monument. On the other hand, preservationists objected to any move at all as the work marked the location of the old City Hall. The decision was made that, yes, the work would be moved, but a plaque would be added recognizing the humiliation and mistreatment of Native Americans. No one was happy: the Indians, the Franciscan fathers and even the government of Spain complained. Eventually semi-acceptable language was cobbled for the plaque. At the time, Mayor Willie Brown said, "I would suggest that the troubles of these times cannot be corrected by a single plaque." Likewise, the events of early California history cannot be depicted in a single monument, but Frank Happersberger sure tried his best.

What's This?

29. Doggie Diner Head

The seven-foot-high Dachshund head impaled on a tall pole in a median strip near what once was its home in front of the Doggie Diner hot dog palace at 46th Avenue and Sloat Boulevard won't mean much to new arrivals to San Francisco. To old-timers, however, it brings alive memories of days spent at Playland at the Beach and Fleishacker Pool that ended with consistently greasy hot dogs and hamburgers at the restaurant.

This particular Doggie Diner—that later became the Carousel Restaurant—was one of the last holdouts when, in the 1980s, the once-prominent chain, unable to compete with McDonald's and the other faster fast-food operations, began to close down its 13 San Francisco outlets. (There had once been 30 "Doggies" in the Bay Area.)

It was not only hamburgers and hot dogs that inspired reverent memories of the Doggie Diners. It was also the welcoming fiberglass dogs heads like this one with its enigmatic smile, halo-like chef's cap, and sporty bow tie that fronted the restaurants. In 2000, this Doggie head became a contentious political issue when the owners of the property wanted to tear down the building, removing the Doggie head and demolishing the Carousel. At the Board of Supervisors, debate raged over whether to give the restaurant and the Doggie head landmark status, which would have made it more difficult for the owners of the property to bulldoze the building and send the head to an ephemera museum. (At the time there were 211 official landmarks in San Francisco, but only two of them—Jack's and Tadich Grill—were restaurants, and they had been around for 100 years.) Attorneys for the property owner argued that "the 30-year-old plastic sign lacks the 'exceptional importance' necessary to landmark an item of such recent vintage."

Some of the supervisors, however, proposed a less restrictive definition of "landmark." "Seventy years from now," said Supervisor Mark Leno, "we might be arguing over whether to landmark the last Starbucks sign."

As things turned out, neither the head nor the Carousel was landmarked. Now the restaurant is gone, but the head remains standing near where it had been. Meanwhile, Doggie Diner heads have turned up in public and private hands throughout the Bay Area. In the city of Emeryville, a Doggie Diner head passed the litmus test to be accepted as public art; another graced an Anderson Valley Ranch known as the Sheep Dung Estates; and on a property in Glen Ellen, the owner arranged his collection of Doggie heads pointing in different directions, just like the mysterious visages scattered around Easter Island.

What's This?

30. Colombo Market Arch

This arch at Front Street and Pacific Avenue is all that's left of the Produce District that, until its displacement by the Golden Gateway redevelopment project in the 1960s, dominated this waterfront location. These days, at 3 o'clock in the morning, things are pretty quiet in the neighborhood. That wasn't the case for many years after the Colombo Market took root here in 1874. Wagons loaded with bell peppers, eggplant, artichokes, rosemary, and sweet basil would be rolling in from farms in the outlying area during the early morning hours.

The growers would have left their homes about midnight traveling by horse-drawn contraptions for three hours or more from their plots on the outskirts of the city at locations such as Lake Merced and the Bayview. As the morning picked up, a dozen languages could be heard haggling over the day's offerings. The retail markets got first shot at the produce, then the hotels and boarding houses. Finally, the ordinary homemakers, if they were patient and waited until about 10 a.m. when things shut down, could buy produce at fire sale prices.

While the activity at the market drew a rich cross section of the San Francisco population, the produce business was the private fiefdom of Genovese Italians. It was the Genovese who grew the produce, sold it at the market, and scraped up the horse droppings left behind to provide fertilizer for the farms. It's been conjectured that the reason San Francisco Italians came to dominate the garbage business was because of the proficiency they developed cleaning up every day at the Colombo Market.

The market thrived for many years. From 1860 on, vegetable growing had been the most profitable business in Northern California. After 1920, growers began shipping produce all over the United States. The growers were also affecting local palates by introducing European exotica such as oregano and thyme to local menus. But the market was a messy place, and by the 1950s too many rats per square meter were residing in what was becoming prime San Francisco real estate.

The forces of urban renewal pounced. This was the era of big government, federally funded projects. "Slum removal" was the order of the day. In the Fillmore District—the Western Addition—the Redevelopment Agency set out to "improve" the vital neighborhood by removing thousands of residents.

Classic, but so-called blighted Victorian homes were bulldozed. The culturally rich Harlem of the West was demolished.

But redevelopment at the produce market was substantially different. The area was less densely populated, and the city provided the market with a new and appropriate site at the southwest end of the city. In its place was to be what the agency called "a new town in town." The Golden Gateway was planned to combine residential, retail, commercial, and open space. Part of the open space created was Sydney Walton Park where the Colombo Market Arch still stands, having escaped the wrecking ball. Perhaps it was Sydney Walton himself, then vice chairman of the Redevelopment Agency, who made the decision to spare the arch. If so, that may be reason enough to name a little park after him.

Why?

31. Why Are San Francisco Fire Hydrants Different Colors?

L et's start with the outlier, the gold-lacquered fire hydrant on 20th Street between Dolores and Church. This relic gets a new coat of paint each April 18 in honor of its role in saving a good piece of the Mission District at the time of the 1906 conflagration that destroyed 25,000 buildings or 80 percent of the city's property value. The Little Hydrant That Could managed to function at a time other hydrants were producing not so much as a trickle. Some 300 breaks in the city's water mains had turned the city's water distribution system into a sieve.

When it was discovered that that the 20th Street hydrant was still functioning—probably because it was drawing its water from an underground spring rather than the city's water supply—300 residents took on the task of propelling fire engines up 20th Street, a task beyond the endurance of the horses that would normally have performed this job. Many homes north of 20th Street are still with us due to this effort.

But the 1906 fire served as a wake-up call for a city that since 1849 had burned to the ground six times. In 1908, City Engineer Marsden Mason vowed to put an end to these infernos. Collecting data from 250 cities throughout the world, he developed the water-abundant system we have today. To the San Francisco pedestrian, the system is most visible by observing what one writer called the "Laurel and Hardy" fire hydrants that dot our Streets. The skinny **white** "Stan Laurel" low-pressure hydrants draw on the city's potable water network. Some of these have been around a very long time as indicated by the ball on top of many of them, meant as tethering points for horses.

But Mason wanted to make sure there was much more. He oversaw the construction of three reservoirs and tanks, all at heights where the gravitational pull would release flow of water to the lowlands. The thick "Oliver Hardy," high-pressure hydrants draw from these storage places. Their colored tops reveal the source of the water: **blue,** a tank on Jones Street; **red,** one on Ashbury, and **black,** the reservoir at Twin Peaks.

Mason still was taking no chances. He constructed 175 underground cisterns, mostly at the center of intersections. These storage sites can provide water for the **green-**headed hydrants nearby. Further, there are two pump stations

located near the bay capable of delivering saltwater to quell out of control flames. Finally, the city's two fireboats are at the ready to pump bay water into the auxiliary water system.

One observer at the time of the 1906 catastrophe wrote, "The earth shook, the sky burned." Given San Francisco's geology, it is highly possible that the earth will shake again, but will the sky burn? That's less likely given the diligence of Marsden Mason and his colleagues following the worst fire ever experienced by an American city.

What Happened Here?

32. Patty Hearst's Hideout

This building at 1827 Golden Gate Avenue is typical of the kind of outlying San Francisco apartment where people have lived more or less ordinary lives since the 1920s. In the early months of 1974, however, activity in one of these studio units was anything but typical. Crowded into this space were all 10 members of the Symbionese Liberation Army (SLA), led by the escaped con, police snitch, and self-appointed revolutionary Donald DeFreeze, who had renamed himself "Cinque," after the leader of a slave ship rebellion. The 11th occupant of the apartment was 19-year-old Patricia Hearst, of the newspaper Hearsts, who had been confined to a closet, blindfolded, and subjected to mind games for eight weeks following her kidnapping in February.

Hearst, a student at the University of California, had been taken by the SLA from her Berkeley apartment. The little band of parlor revolutionaries, planned to use Hearst as a bargaining chip to free two SLA members who had been arrested for the murder of Oakland School Superintendent Marcus Foster. Foster thought he could relieve the violence and chaos in the Oakland schools by issuing student identity cards. The SLA smelled "fascism," and Foster went down. The prisoner exchange plan, however did not work. Then Governor Ronald Reagan was not amenable.

So the SLA went to Plan B. They now approached Patty's father, the increasingly frantic Randolph Hearst, publisher of the *San Francisco Examiner,* with a demand for a massive food giveaway to the poor of California. Hearst's rich friends weren't interested in helping out. Reagan said he would cut off welfare checks to anyone accepting a handout. But Hearst managed to put together $2 million from his own assets, enough to sponsor what turned out to be a badly executed giveaway. Riots broke out, food was stolen, turkeys were thrown from the back of moving trucks as hungry and not so hungry people fought over them. In a taped communiqué Patty told her father, "So far it sounds like you... managed to turn this into a real disaster."

Matters seemed at an impasse. But 59 days into the young Hearst's captivity the other shoe dropped. Patty emerged from her closet to be photographed in full pseudo-revolutionary gear proclaiming herself "Tania" after a female fighter who had died with Che Guevara. Tania said she would stay with the SLA, to fight for her freedom "and for the freedom of oppressed people everywhere."

Unsurprisingly, Patty's conversion was greeted with skepticism by her

family and many others, so Cinque decided he needed to up the ante and put his newly minted revolutionary on public display. On April 15, the little band pulled off a $10,000 bank robbery at the Sunset branch of the Hibernia Bank. Patty was caught on camera with an M1-rifle and wig, announcing, "I am Tania."

Shortly after, Cinque began feeling the heat in San Francisco, so he took his troops to Los Angeles where they were tracked down at their bungalow hideout and incinerated in a firefight. Patty was not with her comrades and managed to stay on the run for more than a year before being captured at an apartment near the Cow Palace.

For her trial, on bank robbery charges, her father hired showboat attorney F. Lee Bailey, who passed up chances for a plea that might have resulted in probation, in favor of a "brainwashing" defense. The jury was not convinced. Patty was convicted and the judge sentenced her to 14 years in prison. After seven years her sentence was commuted by President Jimmy Carter. In 2001, President Bill Clinton granted her a full pardon.

Why Is This There?

33. Coit Tower

At the peak of Telegraph Hill, the 189-foot-tall Coit Tower rises above the 288-foot crest, providing the San Francisco skyline with one of its most dramatic and memorable features. The structure is with us today because of a rather imprecise bequest to the city by one Lillie Hitchcock Coit.

Coit, the daughter of an Army surgeon, came to the city as a child in 1851. A key event of Coit's childhood was her experience with a fire in a vacant house where she was playing with some of her friends. She escaped; two of her friends did not.

It was probably because of this incident that Coit developed an early attachment to firemen and their work. In the days before motorized fire engines, she joined firefighters in the arduous task of pushing and pulling the horse-drawn fire wagons up Telegraph Hill.

Lillie's admiration for firefighters may have led her to adopt many of the characteristics of the men who did this work. She wore pants, smoked cigars, and played poker. In 1861, despite these idiosyncrasies, she married Howard Coit, a caller at the San Francisco stock exchange and well-attached in the community of San Francisco's movers and shakers. The marriage was not made in heaven. Lillie continued her edgy life filled with gambling, guns and decidedly unfeminine behavior until Coit died in 1885 at age 47.

With the demise of her husband, Lillie packed up and went to France where she attached herself to the court of Napoleon III. There her eccentricities were appreciated to a degree they had not been when she moved among San Francisco's upper crust. She continued to live in Europe off and on until 1929 when she returned to San Francisco where she died.

Before she left for Europe, however, Coit had expressed a desire to do something special for the city that had been her first home. Upon her death she left $118,000 to be "expended in an appropriate manner for the purpose of adding to the beauty of the city which I have always loved."

Those vague instructions left the city fathers with a lot of latitude. Park Commissioner and Board of Supervisors member Herbert Fleishhacker remembered Coit's connection to Telegraph Hill. Beautification of the hill, he successfully argued, was how the money should be spent. But what form would this beautification take?

Of the plans that were submitted, the one that rose to distinction was proposed by the firm of Arthur Brown Jr., who was responsible for the development of much of San Francisco's Civic Center. Brown's fluted tower is not intended to resemble a fire nozzle, an urban myth with which some tour guides still entertain unsuspecting tourists. Brown, in fact, said the tower is intended to resemble nothing at all.

What would Lillie Coit have thought of this particular way of "adding beauty to the city?" Her friend, author Gertrude Atherton, who herself found the tower to be "an insult to the landscape," thought she knew. "Lillie had an aversion to towers," she said.

Why Are These There?

34. Coit Tower Murals

T his is Victor Arnautoff's depiction of *City Life,* one of the Coit Tower murals which were executed by 26 artists employed in 1934 by the federally funded Public Works of Art Project (PWAP). The murals are there because of a confluence of circumstances that touched off a bit of an arts explosion at the top of Telegraph Hill. The tower, a gift of Lillie Hitchcock Coit, had, in 1933, lurched to completion after warding off detractors, some of whom asked, "What is this thing going to be good for?"

Back then, San Francisco had attracted a group of artists who had been influenced by Diego Rivera and other Mexican muralists of the 1930s. The arts also had friends in President Franklin D. Roosevelt's administration who were looking for ways to put artists to work during the catastrophic Great Depression as well as to visually advance the values of Roosevelt's New Deal.

So when Dr Walter Heil, director of the de Young Museum, got word from Washington that the administration wanted him to chair PWAP activities out West, and to make plans to find "worthy artists" to "embellish" appropriate buildings, he knew just which building should be first embellished and who the artists should be to carry out the task. Now the tower would have a purpose.

The assembled artists quickly agreed on a palette and a scale as well as subject matter for the murals: "contemporary Americana life in all its aspects." They also chose a medium—fresco—the preferred art-making technique of the Mexican muralists. The fresco artist renders a work in watercolor on wet plaster so the colors penetrate and become fixed. The effect is to provide a radiant glow. The result of all this agreement was to create a uniformity among the works that leaves the impression that many could have been created by a single artist.

While the production of the murals went off smoothly, the aftermath was anything but smooth. This was the year of the maritime strike that pitted the International Longshoremen's Association against the waterfront employers. Residents were choosing up sides, and the side the major newspapers had chosen was that of the employers. Suspicious of the radical politics of some of the muralists, the papers unleashed their newshounds to find evidence of subversion. Most of the murals emphasizing California industry, agriculture, and city life were devoid of political content. By cherry-picking, the papers found what they were looking for: a copy of Karl Marx's *Das Kapital* here, an issue of

the leftist *The New Masses* there.

More blatantly, one of the artists, Clifford Wight, had executed the symbol of Russian communism: a hammer and sickle accompanied by the words "Workers of the World Unite." Wight explained that this rendering was part of tableau of "alternatives" that included symbols of capitalism and of Roosevelt's New Deal. But the powers that be weren't buying his explanation. In July, the city shut down Coit Tower, offering the excuse that "someone might throw rocks or give signals" to the waterfront below during the labor crisis. In October, the strike was settled, and the tower reopened, but the Wight work had disappeared, never to be accounted for. Since then the murals have undergone other tribulations. Indeed, by 1960, the works had been vandalized to the point where access was closed to the public until they were restored in 1977.

When Dr. Heil heard that the artists planning the murals were intending to work in fresco, he was truly excited. Thinking of the frescos of ancient Egypt and Greece that are still with us, he said, "These may last 1,000 years." This may not be impossible, if the citizens of San Francisco can stay focused on preserving these exceptional creations for the next millennium or so.

Who's This?

35. Philo T. Farnsworth

Here's Philo T. Farnsworth, immortalized in bronze at George Lucas's Digital Arts Center in San Francisco's Presidio. He's right at home because it was at 202 Green Street, at the foot of Telegraph Hill, that Farnsworth invented television. Arriving in San Francisco in 1927, as a 21-year-old, barely adult, Farnsworth put to work his "dissector unit." One day he was able to transmit an image from one room of his Green Street lab to another. A confident young man, he told his colleagues, "That's it folks, there you have electronic television."

In fact, Farnsworth had been mulling over this invention for seven years. At 14 he was plowing his father's potato field in Idaho when he noticed the furrows lined up in neat parallel rows. For the rest of us, a furrow is a furrow is a furrow, but the young Farnsworth saw something else. He saw the furrows as lines in a picture that could be broken down, transmitted, then reassembled into a complete picture. Just like television.

Shortly after this epiphany, Farnsworth was fortunate to come upon the well-connected George Iverson, who lobbied the Crocker Bank in San Francisco to fund the young genius to the tune of $25,000 plus use of the Green Street lab. But Farnsworth's embryonic beginnings were not producing a marketable product. As the initial grant depleted, a man from the Crocker Bank showed up at Green Street asking for a demonstration. "When are we going to see the dollars in this thing?" he wanted to know. As if on cue, Farnworth's assistant slid an image in front of the image dissector in one room, and, on the glowing blue screen in the adjoining room, appeared a thick black dollar sign. The banker could now see his dollars. More support from the bank was forthcoming.

By 1929, Farnsworth was transmitting visual signals to the Hobart Building a mile away. Word about this world-changing invention was getting out, and prominent visitors began to find their way to Green Street. Among them was David Sarnoff, the president of RCA. Sarnoff's people had also been tinkering with a primitive television, but what he saw in Farnsworth's lab was much closer to a real product than anything he had on the drawing board. But, not showing his cards, Sarnoff left Green Street saying, "There's nothing here we'll need."

Sarnoff later offered Farnsworth $100,000 for his patents. But the inventor rejected the offer, not only because it was a puny sum considering what he had

to sell, but because his role model, Thomas Edison, had not sold his patents. Like Edison, Farnsworth wanted to establish licensing agreements.

By 1931, the Green Street operation was bleeding red ink, and Farnsworth picked up and went to work for RCA in Philadelphia. A few years later, Sarnoff brazenly sued Farnsworth over 14 patents. Sarnoff lost, and, in 1939, had to pay Farnsworth a million dollars for the rights to his main patents. By then, however, drinking and depression were taking their toll on Philo Farnsworth. He lingered until 1971, dying flat broke and largely forgotten. Yet the eastern end of Green Street can still boast of being a home to "the most influential unknown person of the 20th century."

Why?

36. Why Is the Golden Gate Bridge Painted Orange?

A Golden Gate Bridge should be golden, right? Well, not necessarily. The "Golden Gate" here refers to the strait, the entrance to San Francisco Bay from the Pacific Ocean. Army Captain John C. Fremont gave the strait its name in 1846 because he said it reminded him of the entrance to Istanbul harbor, the Golden Horn.

Irving Morrow, the designer who gave the bridge its art deco look and lighting, did not want the bridge's color pallette to be limited by this historical baggage. One day he came upon a painter applying an orangish undercoat to one of the bridge's towers and had an epiphany. That was the color he wanted. The hue blended just right with the warm colors of the Marin hills on the north side of the bridge and complemented the gray fog that rolled in almost daily. He settled on "International Orange" and prepared a 29-page memo to that effect, convincing a skeptical bridge Board of Directors.

The color also provides better visibility for passing ships than the generic gray that was the bridge color *de jour*, though not quite as much as the black with yellow stripes that the U.S. Navy would have preferred or the white and red that was the Army Air Corps' favorite. International Orange is specially mixed for the bridge district. And, no, it is not true, as you may have heard, that the bridge is painted each year from end to end. It is continually being painted here and there as needed.

What Happened Here?

37. The East Side of Telegraph Hill

Around the turn of the last century, the San Francisco Merchants Association described this eastern slope of Telegraph Hill as "scared, gashed, dismantled, and forlorn." As one can see, except for the hearty survival of a few recently planted native succulents, not much has changed.

This sorry tableau is the singular creation of George and Harry Gray, who engaged in unfettered quarrying of the hill for about 20 years starting in the 1890s. The Grays' operation was supply-and-demand capitalism gone wild. The city needed rock—land was being filled, roads were being built. The Grays had the facilities to supply it, not only with their Telegraph Hill operation, but also with their quarries at Noe Valley and Corona Heights.

Despite their name, "Gray," there was nothing nuanced about these genuinely bad apples. They made no bones about their for-profit attack on the hill, ignoring the complaints of the neighborhood's Irish and Italian immigrants whose small homes would tumble down the hillside after a quarry blast.

In their destructive efforts the brothers were abetted by the corrupt city government. The Grays, along with many other business owners who needed the city of San Francisco to turn a blind eye, were the clients of political boss Abe Ruef. It should have been no surprise when the Ruef-controlled Board of Public Works declared that only blue-type rock found exclusively on the Gray's holdings could be used in public projects.

The beginning of the end for the Grays came when two civic-minded women, Alice Griffith and Elizabeth Ashe, formed an organization called "The Willing Circle" to improve conditions in the neighborhood. At the top of their agenda was the campaign to stop the destruction of Telegraph Hill. Also involved in the effort was Dr. Dorthea Moore, who was not shy about announcing that the ladies were "a little group of fanatics."

Hill residents—originally distrustful of females, WASPs, and outsiders—came to recognize the efforts of these women, and their work gained the support of civic leaders and newspapers in what was the beginning of the San Francisco environmental movement. Politicians were pressured to order the quarrying to stop in 1903. That should have been the end of it, but it wasn't. The Grays continued to blatantly violate the law, going so far, in 1909, as to cause one of their blasts to coincide with the firing of the Fourth of July cannons at the Presidio.

No one was fooled.

In the end, it was the Gray brothers' greed that did them in. They had made a practice of cheating their workers. In 1909 an unpaid employee shot and killed the Grays' cashier. Not learning from this experience, George Gray met his demise when he was gunned down by Joe Lococo, a former quarry worker desperate to feed his family, to whom Gray refused to pay $17.50 in back wages. A jury, in a measure of just how well the Grays were regarded in the community, found Lococo not guilty by reason of temporary insanity.

After that the Grays' enterprise took a nose dive. By 1914, the firm was bankrupt and the destruction of the hill had stopped. But the damage had been done. In 1927, the press reported, "A slide of earth and rock plunged down Telegraph Hill. Numerous small structures, chicken houses and fences were swept tumbling and smashing under the sea of mud, boulders and debris." Even now, each winter, hill residents face the possibility that mud slides will force them to evacuate their homes. Shakespeare was right about the evil that men do living after them.

What's This?

38. The Columbarium

This is the Columbarium, off Anza Street in the Richmond District, one of the few places in San Francisco where human remains have been preserved unmolested. The Columbarium, with its thousands of niches, built in 1898 by the OddFellows Fraternal Organization, came on line at an appropriate time to take on the burgeoning overpopulation of the dead.

When the structure was erected, San Francisco, and the Richmond District in particular, were being overwhelmed by the remains of the nonliving, estimated to be as many as 200,000. Realizing the city has only 40 some square miles to work with and a lot of dead people taking up a big piece of this space, the Board of Supervisors said enough corpses were enough. In 1914, they decreed that all remains (except, of course, those tucked away in the Columbarium), would be removed from city cemeteries.

In a process that took decades, bodies were transported to the town of Colma, five miles south of San Francisco, which now has the distinction of being the only American city where the dead outnumber the living.

Remains still do rest at a couple of cemeteries in San Francisco. There's the National Cemetery in the Presidio You need to be a U.S. military veteran to go underground at this location, and the remaining spots are spoken for, though a few Important Personages such as Representative Phillip Burton—who, after all, fathered the Golden Gate National Recreation Area of which the Presidio is part—have been allowed in.

A historic but dinky cemetery (140 feet by 60 feet) can be found on the site of Mission Dolores. Established in 1776, the date of the mission's founding, the last burial took place here in the 1870s. Time and vandalism have damaged the site, but important people in the early history of our city reside here, including early Californians whose memories are celebrated by street names in the surrounding Mission District: Guerrero, Valencia, Sanchez, and Noe. Film buffs will know this location as the site where Kim Novak visits the grave of her presumed body double, Carlotta Valdes, in the Hitchcock film, *Vertigo*.

For others, the Columbarium is still fulfilling its function, now under the auspices of the Neptune Society, of allowing dedicated San Franciscans to stay put in the city they love.

Why?

39. Why Are All Those Flags in Front of the Fairmont Hotel?

Count 'em. There should be 50, representing each of the 50 nations that signed on to attend the 1945 international conference to draft a charter for the United Nations. These 50 nations, all of which had been at war with Hitler and the Japanese, saw the UN as their best hope to establish a world that protects international security and respects human rights.

The flags reside above the Fairmont's entrance because, although ceremonial sessions for the emerging organization took place at the War Memorial Opera House and its neighbor, the Veteran's Building, much of the grunt work involved in drafting the charter occurred in the Garden Room of the hotel. Many delegates stayed at the hotel, and it was here that President Harry Truman spent the night before the celebratory conclusion of the conference on June 26, 1945.

The San Francisco site had been settled on by Winston Churchill, Joseph Stalin, and Franklin D. Roosevelt, the leaders of Great Britain, the USSR and the United States, the "Big Three" opponents of the Axis powers. Why San Francisco? The answer is not quite clear. Secretary of State Edward Stettinius said something about "feeling the fresh air of the Pacific." It is known that Roosevelt, who died before the conference convened, wanted to shift attention away from Europe and toward the Pacific Rim. The San Francisco site also worked well for the often recalcitrant Russians. Rather than cross through an active war zone as would be necessary if the meeting were held in, say, New York, they could just hop over to Seattle from their east coast, then south to the city.

San Franciscans were surprised and delighted to host the event, though they needed to scamper to pull it off. San Francisco was not yet a conventioneers destination, and the city fathers needed to move fast to accommodate 3,500 attendees—the representatives of 80 percent of the world's population—as well as 2,500 members of the press and other observers. Apparently few were disappointed. One reporter for the Associated Press wrote, "San Francisco is one of the great and wonderful cities of the world." Not only that, but delegates will "see more cocktail bars than probably in all their lives before, and they'll laugh at the dinky jam-packed cable cars, festooned with human beings hanging on the outside as they bump over the hills. They can also take a gander at the real live leg art in one of those places whose blazing red signs announce 'burlesque.' "

The delegates were up to much more than fun and games. As President Truman told their assembly at its final session, "You have created a great instrument for peace, security and human progress in the world." A million men had been transported through San Francisco to fight the war; now in 1945, the city was at the center of a world hoping for peace.

What's This?

40. Immigration Station at Angel Island

These barracks at Angel Island are what remains of the so-called Ellis Is-land of the West. From early in the 20th century to the 1940s, the island's wooden buildings were the first home of many new arrivals entering America from the Pacific. Some of these immigrants included Australians, New Zealanders, Canadians, and Europeans, traveling first and second class. These folks would, as a rule, have their papers processed aboard ship and be allowed to disembark.

Not so for the Chinese arrivals. Since the Chinese Exclusion Act of 1882, the federal government, acting on the demands of western politicians and a California population fearful of job loss, made every effort to keep out Chinese immigrants. When Chinese arrived on the island, they were confined at this supposedly escape-proof location, unable to communicate with anyone on the mainland.

Chinese seeking to make it off the island had to find a loophole. Some professions were exempt from exclusion: merchants, clergy, diplomats, and students. Also children of American-born Chinese were allowed to enter. When the 1906 earthquake and fire struck, the Chinese immigrants caught a break. Municipal records had been destroyed in the conflagration, so it was no longer possible to identify which residents were born in the United States. The phenomena of "paper sons"—and sometimes "paper daughters"—emerged in which "native born" Chinese residents of the mainland would claim an immigrant as a son or daughter. Immigration officials, however, were not easily stymied. They subjected the new arrivals to intense interrogation, lasting several hours or even days, in which the applicant would be asked detailed questions about family history, location of their villages, and more. To survive this process, the immigrant and the sponsor would have to collude, getting their answers in synch, as the sponsor would also undergo interrogation and any discrepancy could mean deportation for the immigrant.

In a time before modern communications, this confirmation could be a lengthy process and immigrants remained under lock and key for 24 hours a day. All the conditions of a substandard prison, from a firetrap structure to inedible food, were very much in evidence.

When the Immigration Station's administration building burned to the ground in 1940, the Angel Island station was closed. Then in 1943, as the

United States and China became World War II Allies, the Chinese Exclusion
Act was repealed, and Chinese were allowed to become naturalized citizens—
though until 1965 only 105 Chinese were allowed to enter each year.

Today, Angel Island is administered by the National Park Service and the
Immigration Station has undergone historic renovation. But some poems of
former residents scrawled on the walls remain. Part of one reads:

> *Nights are long and the pillow cold; who can pity my loneliness*
>
> *After experience such loneliness and sorrow,*
>
> *Why not just return home and learn to play the fields?*

Who's This?

41. Harvey Milk

This bust of Harvey Milk, one of the nation's first openly gay elected officials, has been a fixture outside the Supervisors' Chambers at City Hall since 2008. The piece stands in contrast to the other bronzed visages that grace the building. For one thing, Milk is the only person so honored who was not a mayor. He was, rather, a city supervisor. He is also the only one who is smiling.

That's an appropriate pose, because although Milk was engaged in exceedingly serious business, he almost always seemed to be in good spirits. Recognized as his high school class clown, he retained an impishness that, combined with an adaptive intelligence, allowed him early on to fit into jobs as diverse as a Wall Street researcher and diving instructor in the U.S. Navy.

Arriving in San Francisco in the 1960s when the city had come to prominence as having the highest per capita gay population in the nation, Milk, the former campaigner for Barry Goldwater, began to shed his past. Outraged by the Vietnam War, he let his hair grow long, losing his job at an investment firm as a result. His home was San Francisco until the day in 1978 when he, along with Mayor George Moscone, was shot dead at City Hall by former Supervisor Dan White.

Earlier, in 1973, acting with the impulsiveness that characterized many of his decisions, he used his last $1,000 to open a camera shop after a roll of film he had left at another shop had been ruined.

Milk's political awakening had little to do with gay rights. Rather, he was consumed by a more general sense of injustice. The little stuff was getting to him: a state bureaucrat came to his store dunning him with what he considered an unfair tax payment; a teacher dropped by asking to borrow a movie projector because the equipment at her school did not function. The government's priorities, he came to believe, were out of whack. "I finally reached the point where I knew I had to become involved or shut up."

It turned out he was a natural politician. In four political campaigns—three failing ones before his successful supervisorial run—he was able to put together a coalition of firefighters, construction workers, gay men, liberal types and Irish grandmothers. The assistant campaign manager at his camera shop campaign headquarters was an 11-year-old girl.

HARVEY MILK

An ebullient campaigner, Milk may have invented what has become a ubiquitous low-rent campaign strategy. He would bulk up dozens of supporters at Market Street intersections waving Harvey Milk placards.

In 1977, after San Francisco voters decided to replace citywide election of supervisors with representatives elected from districts, Milk, "The Mayor of Castro Street," as he had seemingly dubbed himself, was elected from San Francisco's gayest neighborhood. He now fully accepted a role as a bellwether in the Gay Revolution. He likened himself to Jackie Robinson, saying, "You can sit around and throw bricks at Silly Hall or you can take it over. Well, here we are."

Milk began his tenure by successfully sponsoring what was to be the nation's most encompassing law protecting gays against discrimination. But he was also a fix-the-potholes kind of guy. When he learned that San Franciscans considered dog excrement the town's No. 1 problem, he sponsored a law requiring dog owners to scoop their pets' feces, known as the "pooper-scooper" law. With his usual flair for the dramatic, he invited the media to a press conference in Duboce Park to explain the ordinance, where, with cameras rolling. he "accidentally" stepped in a pile of pre-arranged doggie doo.

Milk's greatest legacy may be in his insistence that progress in gay civil rights was inexorably linked to the willingness of gays to come out: "Gay doctors . . . gay lawyers . . . gay judges and architects. I hope that every professional gay will say 'enough,' come forward and tell everybody, wear a sign. Let the world know, maybe that will help."

Why Is This There?

42. Grace Cathedral

G race Cathedral, the magnificent structure occupying the Nob Hill block between California, Sacramento, Jones, and Taylor Streets, dominates this proud location because of the generosity of the heirs of Charles Crocker, one of the builders of the transcontinental railroad. In the 1870s, he had built a "wedding cake" of a mansion on this site. In 1920, the family donated the property to the Grace Episcopal Church. But the location carries with it historical baggage that has little to do with Christian charity.

Along with Leland Stanford, Mark Hopkins, and Collis Huntington—his colleagues in the railroad enterprise—Crocker's wheeling and dealing had made him hugely rich. Collectively, "The Big Four," as the quartet was known, was worth billions in today's currency. With no cash flow problem, they were soon thrashing about for ways to spend their money. Seemingly in tandem, all four settled on the idea to build showplace residences at the crest of Nob Hill. The recently inaugurated cable car line to the top of the hill made sites in this area more desirable and more expensive to procure. For these tycoons though money was no object. Each of them set out to buy an entire city block whatever the price. Other very rich men got in on the act, too. James Flood, who had made his money in silver, not railroads, for instance, paid the then substantial sum of $25,000 for the property at 1000 California Street, and built the structure that is today's Pacific Union Club.

Crocker, however, was of a different breed. He lived by his lifelong motto: "Never spend a dime when you can get it for a nickel." He was eager to one-up his colleges with a four-story, 100-room mansion that would advertise his wealth, if not his good taste, but he wasn't going to burn unnecessary cash in the process. He began anonymously acquiring the land for his chosen site. All went well until he approached one Nicholas Yung. He was a successful German undertaker who had changed his name when he got tired of people mispronouncing his given surname, "Jung." Since 1855, Yung and his family had lived in relatively isolated contentment in a home on a corner lot that offered stunning views in all directions. Crocker wanted that property. He offered Yung $6,000. Yung, remembering what Flood had paid for a similar property, demanded $12,000.

That was too much for Crocker. He carried out his threat to build a 40-foot "spite" fence, isolating the Yungs' home on three sides. Life for the Yungs

CATHEDRAL

became difficult. All sunlight and airflow was cut off. Plants died. They had to light candles in the daytime. The family finally picked up their home and moved it to a property they owned on Broderick Street. But the Yungs held on to the Nob Hill land and the fence remained. Nicholas Yung died in 1880, and the property passed to his wife, Rosina Yung, who was also unwilling to sell. She said that Crocker was fortunate that she did not take up offers to install a Chinese laundry on the premises. Crocker died in 1888. Then Mrs. Yung died in 1902. Her heirs finally let the Crocker estate have the land in 1904. But there was no need to take down the fence. The fire following the earthquake of 1906 took care of that, obliterating both the fence and Crocker's ostentatious residence. The bickering ended and the land eventually became Episcopal property.

Today seekers of inner peace walk a labyrinth at Grace Cathedral, an exercise from which both Charles Crocker and Nicholas Yung might have benefited.

Red arrow denotes "spite" fence.

43. Harding Park

There's a special reason that this golf course, located on the west end of the city, is named Harding Park. Designed in 1925 by golf club designer Willie Watson, the facility honors the then recently deceased president of the United States, Warren G. Harding, who had breathed his last in San Francisco at the Palace Hotel two years before. In late July 1923, Harding and his imperious wife Florence, appropriately nicknamed "The Duchess," returning from a trip to Alaska, checked into the Presidential Suite of the Palace. Harding was not feeling well. At 58, he was hearty, handsome, gentle, and not very bright. His wife was the brains in the family. It was thought the president only had some kind of bug, but the city was concerned. News vendors outside the hotel hawked the updates of his condition. Mayor "Sunny Jim" Rolph ordered the streetcars on Market Street to stop clanging their bells when they passed the hotel. But, a few days later, on August 2, the president was dead.

Although Harding's death was officially ruled a heart attack, no one knows for sure how he died. That's because his wife would not allow an autopsy on his body. He may have fallen victim to complications from food poisoning he had endured in Alaska, although no one else in his party who had ingested the same meals had fallen ill. He may, indeed, have died of a heart attack, perhaps brought on by high blood pressure exacerbated by worry over well-founded rumors of corruption in his administration.

Or, as some still think, his wife may have done him in. Harding had been a sexual player when the press did not go out of its way to catalogue such indiscretions. He was a man with more than one mistress and at least one out-of-wedlock child to his credit. The strong willed "Duchess" did not take kindly to these shenanigans.

On the early evening of his death, the president seemed to be feeling better. Mrs. Harding had been reading to him. She left the room suddenly and minutes later the president was dead, leaving behind a grist of implications for conspiracy theorists. Within a year, Florence Harding herself had died.

How Did These Get Built?

44. Fontana East and West

These are the Fontana apartments, the 17-story structures that went up in the 1960s. They have served ever since as a Chinese wall disconnecting Russian Hill from Aquatic Park, obliterating views of the bay. How did this happen?

A *San Francisco Examiner* editorial from the '60s provides a pretty good summary of the motivation behind the project: "Basic city policy provides that tall apartments should be limited where feasible to hilltops, the building heights graduating downward as the slopes descend. The policy is sound, *but neither inviolate nor eternal; it cannot be because San Francisco has no direction to grow except upward.*" (Emphasis added).

Not everyone was onboard. Leading the fight against the construction of the Fontana was future Reagan Secretary of Defense Caspar Weinberger, who, in 1961, was the attorney for the Russian Hill Improvement Association. Weinberger, it turns out, was not nearly as successful at putting the brakes on the Fontana plans of developer Peter Mattei as he was at causing the Russians to think again.

When Fontana West was completed and neighbors saw what Mattei had wrought, even greater numbers joined the protest against the construction of Fontana East. Mattei was conciliatory. He said that if he had lived on Russian Hill, he, too, would have joined the protest. Fontana East was finished in 1965 and, in fact, provided a mixed blessing.

Anti-development activists now had a poster child representation for what the waterfront should not be. Today a 40-foot height limit is imposed between Aquatic Park and Telegraph Hill.

45. Harry Bridges Plaza

I n 1999, this space in front of the Ferry Building was christened Harry Bridges Plaza after the President of the International Longshore and Warehouse Union (ILWU), who, from the 1930s to 1950, orchestrated a series of waterfront strikes. If Bridges were still around he might be looking on the passing parade with his characteristic enigmatic expression that often broadened into a quizzical smile. This demeanor, combined with his plain speech, soft delivery, and dulcet tones, had a way of infuriating his opponents across bargaining tables.

But the bosses' main problem with Bridges was that he was both irascible and incorruptible in a way that made him a very tough cookie. His square one premise was, "We the workers have nothing in common with the employers." Meanwhile, he was educating maritime workers on their common bond. "The most important word in the language of the working class is 'solidarity,' " he would say.

Bridges discovered whose side he was on when, as a 13-year-old in Melbourne, Australia, his property owning father sent him out to collect rents from poor families, many unable to pay. "No person with any sensitivity to suffering

Harry Bridges leads the longshoremen in the 1939 Labor Day parade.

could have collected these rents and not had his opinion colored by the task," he said. Bridges left Melbourne and went to sea. In 1920 he jumped ship in San Francisco and went to work on the docks. Here he learned firsthand of the speedups, the corrupt hiring practices, the low wages, and sometimes 24-hour work shifts that created the grievances that culminated in the 83-day West Coast maritime strike of 1934. Bridges led this walkout and was subsequently elected president of the ILWU, a position he held for 40 years.

To the ship owners and their allies, Bridges was increasingly *bête noir* No. 1. For 20 years they worked unsuccessfully to have him deported as an alien and locked up as a Communist who, by definition then, advocated the overthrow of the government. Bridges always denied he was a party member. He certainly had no interest in Communist theorizing. "The union is fighting for things right before our eyes like a 15-cent wage raise, not some complex theory," he said.

In addition to promoting bread-and-butter issues, Bridges organized a union that was truly democratic. Enthusiastic debate was an expected feature of ILWU conclaves, and all decisions were made by a vote of the membership. For much of his tenure, Bridges drew a salary of $40 a week, the typical wage of a longshoreman working the docks.

By the 1950s, the shipowners had tired of the continuing waterfront strife, and Bridges became less sure that management and labor always needed to be at each other's throats. In 1960, the union negotiated a groundbreaking agreement that permitted extensive mechanization of the docks, reducing the number of longshore workers in return for generous job guarantees and benefits for those displaced by the change. A few years later, Mayor Joseph Alioto appointed this one-time "Joseph Stalin of American shipping" to the Port Commission. When he retired in 1977, Bridges received praise not only from the president of Matson Lines, but from Nelson Rockefeller, Republican vice president of the United States. When Bridges died in 1990, Mayor Art Agnos ordered the city's flags flown at half staff.

Bridges would have taken this honor in stride. He once said, "When an old bastard like me retires, people say, 'He's not so bad after all.' "

What's This?

46. Kezar Stadium Gate

This replica of the original concrete arch with the inscription "Kezar Stadium" is all that remains of the venerable structure that housed the birthing of the San Francisco 49ers. Located at the southeastern corner of Golden Gate Park, the once 60,000-seat venue now has a capacity of a few thousand and serves as a site for soccer, lacrosse, and cricket competitions as well as high school football games.

The history of Kezar goes way back before the arrival of the 49ers. Unlike modern sports facilities that have taken root to attract professional sport teams, Kezar was built in response to a desire of locals to have a great venue for amateur athletics. The dream became a reality in 1925 thanks to the generosity of the late Mary E. Kezar, who left $100,000 to build a memorial to her pioneer ancestors.

Before the arrival of the 49ers, the site hosted college football teams, as well as the annual East-West Shrine game. The Jim Corbett and Rocky Marciano championship boxing matches were fought there and the annual "Big Game" between Lowell High and Polytechnic would draw as many as 50,000 fans.

In 1946, trucking executive Tony Morabito paid the All-American Football Conference $25,000 to establish the San Francisco 49ers with a home at Kezar. Truth be told, Kezar was never the ideal venue for pro football. Where else in the league could a punt returner lose a football in the fog? Further, the stands at Kezar were right up against the field. This provided fans an on-top-of-the-action opportunity to listen to quarterback Y. A. Tittle bark out signals, but also for the early Forty Niner Faithful to direct obscenities and missiles onto the field.

In 1947, the 49ers donned uniforms of red and gold—which are still their colors—and embarked on a series of seasons more notable for much-loved players—Frankie Albert, Billy Wilson, Hugh McElherney, Joe Perry and John Brodie—than for playoff-quality performance.

Old-time fans can recall a sad day in 1957 when owner Morabito fell dead of a heart attack while watching a game against the Chicago Bears. When Morabito was struck down, the Niners trailed the Bears 17-7. Dedicating themselves to "win one for Tony," the team pulled off a 21-17 comeback win.

By the 1960s, attendance at the Kezar games had fallen steadily. In 1967, *Ramparts* magazine editor Edward Keating rented the stadium for $250 to hold a peace rally. The event drew more than 50,000, a far larger crowd than the 49ers had seen for some time. In 1970, the 49ers played their last game at Kezar, moving their operation to Candlestick Park where the team experienced many seasons of exhilarating highs and depressing lows, while planning its exit to the city of Santa Clara in 2014.

Who's This?

47. Emperor Norton

Maybe it's because San Francisco has never been much about erecting monuments to its famous and infamous that this representation of one of the city's most celebrated citizens has been relegated to the cozy confines of the Comstock Saloon at Columbus and Pacific.

The work, by Peter Macchiarini, is a fanciful likeness of Norton I, self-proclaimed Emperor of the United States and Protector of Mexico.

Joshua Norton was not born to royalty, rather his eminence evolved. As a 30-year-old Englishman he emigrated from South Africa to San Francisco in 1848, where he resisted the gold fever of '49 and instead bought city real estate that he parleyed into holdings worth a quarter of a million dollars.

No more immune to greed than the rest of the Gold Rush arrivals, however, Norton saw an opening to get even richer. Out of a need to feed its own people, China had stopped exporting rice. Rice, of course, was a staple of the growing San Francisco population. When Norton got hold of a shipload of rice from Peru the path toward greater wealth via a rice monopoly seemed unobstructed. That plan worked for a couple of days until three more shiploads of rice from Peru arrived. The bottom fell out of the rice market, and Norton was ruined.

PHOTO · MIKE LEON

Like many another debtor hounded by his creditors, Norton made the sensible decision to disappear for a few years. He returned to the city in 1857, decked in full military regalia. He mounted the stairs to the offices of the *San Francisco Bulletin* and handed the editor a proclamation: "At the preemptory request and desire of a large number of the citizens of the United States," he had been called on to serve as Emperor, calling together representatives to "ameliorate the evils under which the country is laboring."

The *Bulletin's* editor, George Fitch, recognizing that craziness can sell papers, published Norton's proclamation the next day under the headline: "Have We an Emperor Among Us?" And the 21-year career of Imperial Majesty Emperor Norton I was off and running. Emperor Norton was a different kind of madman. He had opinions on all subjects and, as one observer noted, "His opinions are usually correct, except when related to himself."

Perhaps his proclamation to abolish Congress was a bit of a stretch. Others of his orders seem downright sensible. He issued instructions to form a League of Nations. He ordered a bridge be built from San Francisco to Oakland long before the 1936 crossing became a reality. He demanded that laws prohibiting Chinese from testifying in court be repealed. His order that "after due and proper warning any one heard to utter the abominable word 'Frisco'—which has no linguistic or other warrant... shall be fined 25 dollars" is still observed by a few dedicated natives.

Emperor Norton looked after his city, reviewing the police and making sure the sidewalks were unobstructed. The city looked after the Emperor, providing him with front-row seats at musical and dramatic events, and outfitting him with spiffy uniforms from the Presidio. He was treated to free meals at local watering holes that in turn advertised his patronage. To make ends meet, he began selling his own scrip, accepted by a surprising number of go-alongers. The notes were to be redeemable at 7 percent in 1880. When early in 1880 Norton collapsed on the street and died, few of his investors felt cheated.

His funeral, which drew 30,000 mourners, was the largest event of its kind ever in San Francisco. Norton I was remembered by Police Chief Patrick Crowley as an Emperor who "had shed no blood, robbed no one and despoiled no country." That was a lot more than could be said of others in his line of business, Crowley said.

What's This?

48. *Transcendence* at A. P. Giannini Plaza

The textbook name for this piece, located at the southeast corner of Kearny and California Streets, is *Transcendence*. Thanks to a rechristening by *Chronicle* columnist Herb Caen, the work soon took on another appellation: *The Banker's Heart*.

The work, by the Japanese sculptor Masayuki Nagare, has been at the center of the A. P. Giannini Plaza since 1971, fronting the Bank of America Building, one-time headquarters of the institution that Giannini founded. Caen, of course, would have known that this labeling of this 200 tons of Swedish granite lacked even a metaphorical connection to the tough, but soft-hearted businessman.

Giannini was, in fact, the rare banker to challenge the notion that banks should only loan money to those who don't need it. In his early years, dealing with farmers as the successful front man for his stepfather's San Francisco produce business, Giannini soon discovered that the contempt bankers had for ordinary people was reciprocated. Leaving the family business at age 31, he got a close look at this mutual distrust when he went to work for Columbus Savings and Loan, a small North Beach bank that he found only wanted to do business with the established neighborhood merchants. So in 1904, he set up his own bank, the Bank of Italy, across the street from Columbus Savings. Right away, he set out to show that his bank would be different. He went door to door in North Beach explaining to residents that their money would be better off with him than being stored in jars and under mattresses.

Giannini's big break came during an otherwise catastrophic time in 1906 when the city was devastated by earthquake and fire. Learning of the disaster in his San Mateo home, he left immediately for the city. Knowing that the fire was approaching, he packed up $80,000 from his vaults, borrowed a wagon from his stepfather's produce business, loaded up the treasure, covered it with oranges and produce as disguise, and returned to his San Mateo home to stash his cache.

A few days later, setting up a stand in the heart of North Beach, on a plank supported by beer barrels, A.P. was back in business. He had two advantages over the competition. Other banks were unable to get into their piping-hot

vaults because if they opened them the money inside would burst into flames. Further, the records of these banks had been destroyed. This was not a problem for A.P. He carried depositors' records in his head.

Giannini went on to create the modern bank as we know it. He was the first to open branches, make small loans, provide home mortgages, and facilitate installment credit. By 1924, his bank had more individual depositors than any other bank in the country. In 1928, the Bank of Italy became the Bank of America.

As a lender, A.P. was always ahead of the curve. He was the banker who first advanced auto loans. He funded the movie industry when other banks thought films were a passing fancy, and he purchased $6 million in bonds that jump-started the building of the Golden Gate Bridge.

In the 1920s, after Giannini opened his bank building headquarters at Powell and Market Streets, "the people's banker" could be seen working on the bank's floor with his colleagues. Giannini had drawn up a list of principles to give his bank direction, one of which stated, "The resources of the bank are not to be used for the enrichment of its officers." When A. P. died in 1949, his worth was $500,000, having given many millions to worthy causes. Current-day Wall Street plutocrats, please note.

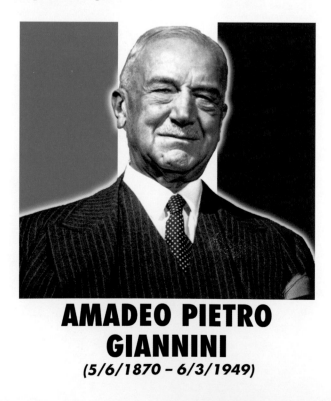

AMADEO PIETRO GIANNINI
(5/6/1870 – 6/3/1949)

What Happened To…?

49. The Embarcadero Freeway

This is the Embarcadero today, minus the Embarcadero Freeway. Typically, San Franciscans are suspicious—if not contemptuous—of any public structure built after 1945. Never has this contempt coalesced as unanimously as with the revulsion directed at the Embarcadero Freeway.

The two-level structure, opened to traffic in 1959, pushed along the Embarcadero for more than a mile, cutting off downtown from the waterfront and isolating the Ferry Building—survivor of the 1906 earthquake—behind a wall of noise and car exhaust.

Then *San Francisco Chronicle* Executive Editor Scott Newhall gave his take on the motivation behind this unfortunate construction: "This awful heirloom rose up out of the rubble of World War II. It was wrought by a naïve generation that had been seized by the delusion that 'bigger,' more brutish, sophomoric, engineering marvels were the bone and sinew of something or other called 'progress.' "

The freeway's snub-nosed termination served as the monument to a citizen's uprising that refused to allow the structure to take a turn inland toward Telegraph Hill and link up with the Golden Gate Bridge. Beyond halting construction, there was little agreement about what should be done with the monolith: Should it be replaced with a tunnel, or housing, or a depressed roadway or a six-lane expressway? Or just spruced up with a few plants to relieve the ugliness?

In 1986, voters even had a chance to make real a plan that came pretty close to what we have now: tear down the freeway and construct a boulevard with jogging paths, bicycle lanes and streetcar lines. But wary voters decided that no change was better than what might be the wrong change.

Then the ante was raised on October 17, 1989. The 6.9 magnitude, 15-second Loma Prieta earthquake (named after its Santa Cruz Mountain epicenter) severely wounded the despised structure. The demolitionists now had a stronger hand to play, and everyone was for removal of the freeway, except those who were against it. Chinatown merchants, in particular, believed that unless the freeway, which provided access to their neighborhood, was restored, their business would tank. Mayor Art Agnos had to step into the contentious debate. Although he had been elected with strong support from Chinatown, he came

down on the side of demolition, saying that the city could not squander "the opportunity of a lifetime." Eventually, he brought the city's supervisors on board.

In February 1991, as fireworks exploded and a group of men in Ethel Merman drag performed an enthusiastic version of "Shake, Rattle and Roll," the demolition began, providing the first step toward the world-class waterfront we have today.

U.S. Senator Dianne Feinstein, who as mayor of San Francisco had shepherded the defeated 1986 plan, was ecstatic. "I knew one day it would happen," she said. "It just needed that push from Mother Nature."

Who's This?

50. St. Francis of Assisi

This is St. Francis of Assisi, a creation of San Francisco sculptor Beniamino Bufano (d. 1970) located in the parking lot of the Longshoreman's Hall at Beach and Taylor Streets. The work, which the late English art critic Roger Fry called, with perhaps a bit of hyperbole, "the most significant piece of sculpture done in 500 years," has found a home at this rather inauspicious location thanks to the intervention of legendary longshoreman union leader Harry Bridges. When Bridges rescued the work, it had been removed from the steps at a seemingly appropriate location, the St. Francis of Assisi Church on Vallejo Street between Grant and Columbus. The congregants had complained that, significant or not, the sculpture got in the way of access during funerals and weddings. At 18-feet high and 12.5 tons, the work probably was a bit out of scale for the modestly-sized church.

But this work was only a sliver of Bufano's St. Francis obsession. He created many other renderings of the saint that can be seen at locations throughout the Bay Area. Among the most memorable is St. Francis of the Guns now on the grounds of City College of San Francisco. After the 1968 killings of Robert Kennedy and Martin Luther King Jr., San Francisco Mayor Joseph Alioto led a voluntary gun turn-in program that accumulated almost 2,000 weapons. Alioto conscripted Bufano to sculpt a St. Francis from the melted guns. On the saint's robe, Bufano created a mosaic depicting four great assassinated American leaders—John and Robert Kennedy, Abraham Lincoln, and King.

Unfortunately, the uber-St. Francis of Bufano's dreams never materialized. It was to be to be a 156-foot steel statue of the saint on horseback placed at the top of Twin Peaks and visible for miles in all directions. It would be a symbol of peace and harmony—a Statue of Liberty for the West Coast. The project planning was spinning right along when Westbrook Pegler, a powerful, if mean-spirited newspaper columnist, found the proposed work violated his pristine taste and mobilized public opinion to defeat the enterprise.

Bufano did not give up on St. Francis, maybe because he lived in emulation of the saint. Like St. Francis the pacifist, Benny renounced war, dining out for years on a questionably true story that he had cut off his trigger finger and sent it to President Woodrow Wilson in protest of World War I. Bufano also shared Francis's lack of interest in worldly goods, living simply, often giving away his work or exchanging his art for food. When he ran out of money, he'd tell friends he was off on an important commission and go down to the Central Valley to pick vegetables.

Bufano also shared with Francis a love of animals. St. Francis, as is well-known, preached to the birds. Bufano created bears, rabbits, seals, and penguins to enrich public spaces throughout this city of St. Francis where, perhaps not surprisingly, there are more dogs than children.

Mayor George Christopher and Beniamino Bufano.

St. Francis of the Guns

Why Is This There?

51. Stevenson Monument

W hy is it that here in Portsmouth Square, in the heart of Chinatown, one finds this tribute to Robert Louis Stevenson, an author firmly anchored in the English white-bread tradition? The answer isn't as off-kilter as one might think. The writer spent many hours in 1879 and 1880 on a bench near this very spot.

Stevenson, a Scotsman, had come to San Francisco in August 1879 seeking the love of his life, Fanny Osborne. She was an American woman 10 years older than he, whom he had met at a writers' colony in France. There was, however, one big problem. Fanny was married with children. When Fanny's husband demanded she return to San Francisco, Stevenson followed not long after. But the Osborne family was now living in Oakland, and Stevenson pined at a residence at 608 Bush Street, waiting for Fanny to finesse a divorce.

Stevenson's health was rickety during these months. He was suffering from tuberculosis, and his melancholy rambles would inevitably take him to Portsmouth Square, where he provided the curious sight of a lanky white man telling stories to Chinese kids. Stevenson was pretty much a literary nonentity who had not yet produced *Dr. Jekyll and Mr. Hyde, Kidnapped, Treasure Island* or the other works that have contributed to his literary immortality.

At the edge of Chinatown he seemed in his element. He had no sympathy with the prevailing prejudice against the Chinese that allowed them to be attacked with impunity and their businesses often destroyed by arson, and he had much respect for their talents. ["The Chinese] were studying the stars before my people learned to keep pigs," he wrote.

Stevenson told his stories in Portsmouth Square until May 1880, when he and Fanny were able to marry. They honeymooned in Napa County before returning to England and a vagabond life that for him alternated between illness and artistic productivity. In 1888, Stevenson and Fanny passed through San Francisco for the last time. They were on their way to the South Seas.

The author died in 1894 at age 44 on the island of Samoa. On hearing of his death, Stevenson's friend Bruce Porter, who headed San Francisco's Guild for Arts and Crafts, decided the writer needed local recognition. Enlisting celebrated architect Willis Polk and sculptor George Piper, the trio created a monument to be located at the writer's favorite dallying place. The final product depicts

a Spanish galleon—a nod to Stevenson's love of the sea. The 9-foot granite
pedestal is inscribed with advice for the "tasks" of life that Stevenson saw as
important: "To be honest and kind . . . not to be embittered." This latter in-
junction could have served as good advice for the creators of the monument.
The Board of Supervisors, exercising their role as community art watchdogs,
rejected Porter and Polk's design as "aesthetically unpleasing." Polk, whose
fame has outlived the passing notoriety of the long forgotten board members,
bit the bullet and made alterations to create the work that has been part of
Portsmouth Square since 1897.

Why Is This There?

52. Fort Point

I t's not difficult to make an educated guess as to why Fort Point is perched on the southern shore of the Golden Gate at the entrance to San Francisco Bay. It's there to protect against aggressors intruding on our space. However, never in its more than 150-year existence has the structure been called on to fulfill this function.

The federal government was alerted to the need for bay defenses shortly after California became American territory in 1848. With the Gold Rush of 1849, a sleepy backwater port was suddenly overwhelmed with ship traffic: 770 vessels that year. There was a chance that some visiting ships would be up to no good. In 1853, the government set out to develop fortifications to protect the bay. In addition to Fort Point, there was to be another fort on the opposite shore, providing the possibility of devastating crossfire to any enemy foolhardy enough to try to bridge this gantlet.

Before Fort Point could be constructed, another task had to be completed. The south shore of the Golden Gate was a 90-foot promontory, useless for artillery that needed to be fired from as close to water level as possible. Workers, in plentiful supply now that disappointed gold seekers had returned to the city, slashed at the bluff, reducing it to 10 feet above sea level.

The model for Fort Point was to be the 30 forts constructed on the East Coast in more or less cookie-cutter-like repetition—think Fort Sumter and Fort McHenry.

California, though, was a long way from Washington, and work proceeded slowly: out of sight, out of mind. Then in 1861, the project got a wakeup call—the Civil War had began, and the fort would be put to use finished or not. Fifty-five guns were mounted, and 500 soldiers were sent to man the facility. The order was given that any vessel flying a rebel flag was to be immediately stopped or "fired into and sunk." But no rebel ships showed up.

There was only one close call. In the summer of 1865, a Confederate raider was known to be on the way to San Francisco. The captain had a plan to run past Fort Point at night, and turn his guns on San Francisco. What he did not know, until informed by a friendly British frigate, was that the war had been over for several months.

The Civil War had also shown that forts like Fort Point could not stand up to new developments in artillery. By 1870, abandonment of Fort Point as a military facility had begun. Since then the fort has occasionally been called into service. During World War II, soldiers stationed there guarded a 6,000-ton 7-mile-long submarine net stretching from Sausalito to San Francisco's Marina.

The closest Fort Point has come to the wrecking ball was in 1937 when

Golden Gate Bridge chief engineer Joseph Strauss latched on to the location as the ideal spot for a huge concrete caisson anchoring the south end of the bridge. After Strauss toured the fort, he changed his mind. "It is a fine example of the mason's art," he said it should be saved. That's what happened in 1970 when President Richard Nixon signed into law a bill establishing the Fort Point National Historic Site.

53. Palace of the Legion of Honor

Viewing this building, those who have visited Paris and its environs will have a nagging feeling that they have been there before. Some San Francisco buildings are a products of the obsession among the city's early 20th-century upper crust with all things French. *Le Petit Trianon* at 3800 Washington Street is a close copy of Marie Antoinette's *pied a terre* at Versailles, for example. The Palace of the Legion of Honor, in particular, grew out of the desire of Alma Spreckels, wife of sugar heir Adolph Spreckels, to notch up a level in San Francisco society that was suspicious of her working-class origins. A trip to France, she thought, would improve her status among the elite.

On the continent, she met a lot of the right people, including sculptor Auguste Rodin from whom she purchased several works on display at the Legion today. She also became friendly enough with French officials that she was able to convince them to open a French Pavilion at San Francisco's Panama Pacific International Exposition in 1915. The pavilion was a replica of the *Palais de la Legion d'Honneur* in Paris. Constructed in the 18th century, the Palais had been

Le Petit Trianon

taken over by Napoleon Bonaparte in 1804 as the home base of the society he created to reward civil and military merit.

Alma Spreckels fell in love with the pavilion and hired prominent local architect George Appelgarth to design a copy that would serve as a museum that she and her husband would present to the city. Appelgarth's palace was a ¾-scale version of the original, but he included several features appropriate to a modern building. Visitors still benefit, for instance, from the hollowed out 21-inch-thick walls which keep temperatures even.

Spreckels chose a beautiful, though remote, site at Lands End for the location of the museum. But there was a problem. Because of the remoteness of the location, the site had been used as a pauper's cemetery from 1868 to 1898. With construction of the Legion, the graves of the deceased were supposed to have been moved to Colma along with others of the dead who had been transported out of San Francisco. When the structure was undergoing retrofitting after the 1989 Loma Prieta earthquake, it was discovered that more than 700 bodies hadn't been moved. Only their name plates had made the journey. The combs, buttons, revolvers, bottles, shoes, safety pins and false teeth that archeologists uncovered during their 1994 dig contrasted with the elegant Legion dominating the site, providing a snapshot of class differences in historic San Francisco.

54. Why Does San Francisco Weather Change From One Block to the Next?

San Francisco environmental writer Harold Gilliam once called attention to the phenomenon of our fickle neighborhood climates: "In New England they say, 'If you don't like the weather wait a few minutes.' " In San Francisco he suggested the more appropriate advice might be, "If you don't like the weather walk a few blocks."

The official name for these rather madding changing weather phenomena is a "microclimate." Without getting too meteorological about it, San Francisco experiences these dramatic climate differences when a chilly sea temperature runs up against a temperate land temperature, creating almost constant breezes that funnel through the gaps, the wind tunnels of the city's hilly topography.

The result: San Francisco may be one of the only cities in the world where a telephone conversation between two residents may begin with, "How's the weather over there?"

Consider a typical summer day when the fog is pouring in from the west, running up against Twin Peaks, Mount Sutro, and Mount Davidson. These ridges hold back the gray onslaught, which, if it makes it over the ridges, heats up and evaporates as it descends. This is why the adjoining areas of the Mission and Noe Valley are known as the city's "banana belt." Similarly, the western neighborhoods—the Sunset, the Richmond, and Pacific Heights—have no protection from the encroaching fog. The incoming fog bank, however, is defeated by the heights of Russian Hill; so North Beach remains sunny.

The fog has a straight shot at the Western Addition and on to downtown where the distribution of wind, fog, and topography leave Nob, Russian, and Telegraph Hills with their own microclimates. Add to this mix the unyielding wind tunnels in the downtown area, the result of our asphalt jungle of high-rises, and we are left with a meteorologist's playground

Fans who followed the San Francisco Giants at Candlestick Park before 1999 knew all about San Francisco's most significant wind tunnel, known locally as the Alemany Gap. The gap provides a free ride for wind and fog from the Sunset District to Candlestick where a couple of wind tunnels collide. Fans at the park were regularly treated to the sight of two stadium pennants,

fully extended, blowing vigorously in opposite directions. These conditions provided a continuing challenge for ball players. At the All-Star Game played at Candlestick in 1961, Giants pitcher Stu Miller was "blown off the mound" in the seventh inning. Miller had thrown a strike, but the umpire was not willing to acknowledge that Miller was working at the epicenter of a 40 mph air quake. He was charged with a balk.

Who's This?

55. Joseph B. Strauss

This is Joseph B. Strauss, the great motivator behind the building of the Golden Gate Bridge. He is depicted in this 5-foot-3, life-sized figure at the south end of the bridge. A man of surpassing ego, drive, and ambition, Strauss took full credit for this wonder of the modern world.

As a young man at the University of Cincinnati, Strauss went out for football and was promptly demolished in practice. While recuperating in the hospital, he vowed to overcome the limitations of his size by becoming the world's greatest bridge builder. His graduate thesis was a design for a bridge linking the United States and Siberia. That plan didn't go anywhere, but he did begin building bridges, including one for the Czar of Russia in St. Petersburg that later laid a claim to fame as one of the key bridges the revolutionaries of 1917 used during the storming of the Winter Palace.

Plying his trade in San Francisco, Strauss designed the Third and Fourth Street bridges, which, while lacking in the aesthetic appeal of the Golden Gate, still provide their work horse function. Strauss's obsession for 20 years, however, was the bridging of the Golden Gate. Unquestionably there was a need. Since the end of World War I, ferries had been busy transporting vehicles across the Golden Gate north to Highway 101.

But the bridge plan met heavy opposition. Some felt a bridge would desecrate the natural opening to the bay; military leaders feared the bridge would be destroyed in wartime; Southern Pacific, the most powerful interest in California, lobbied against the possible disruption of its ferry service. Furthermore, Strauss's 1919 bridge design was ugly. The massive cantilevers on either side connected by a central suspension bridge made his Third Street bridge seem like a paragon of good taste. Strauss, however, was not wedded to the design; it was the spanning of the gate that drove him.

Enthusiastic and confident, for more than a decade he talked up his vision of a mile-long connection across these roaring waters. Strauss once said that it took him two decades and 200 million words to convince people the bridge was feasible, but only four years and $35 million to build it. His salesmanship worked. Regardless of what the engineers, politicians, and economists said, people wanted the Golden Gate Bridge.

More aesthetically astute designers signed onto the project. In 1932, A. P.

Giannini, the founder of the Bank of America, agreed that his bank would buy the bonds necessary to finance its construction; the bridge was off and running. With the bridge being built, Strauss came to rely on the expertise of others. His health was deteriorating, and he spent more and more time in his Nob Hill apartment writing poetry and watching the bridge from afar. Despite his withdrawal, Strauss made sure that he alone was the hero of the day when the bridge was dedicated in May 1937. He died a year later.

Who Thought of This?

56. San Francisco's Pride Parade

I t wasn't a single person, but the San Francisco gay community, who in 1972 decided it was time to parade. That first event was christened "Christopher Street West" in recognition of the riots that had erupted on June 28, 1969, after police raided a gay bar, the Stonewall, on Christopher Street in New York City's Greenwich Village. This watershed event triggered a gay rights movement that resonated widely, particularly in San Francisco.

The next year, the march was rechristened as the Gay Freedom Day Parade. In 1995, understanding the strength in diversity, organizers began calling the event the San Francisco Lesbian, Gay, Bisexual, and Transgender Pride Celebration, the formal title it retains today.

In recognition of its Stonewall beginnings, the parade traditionally takes place on the Sunday morning closest to June 28, along a route from Beale Street, up Market, to Eighth Street. For many years the parade has been led by Dykes on Bikes (formally known as the Women's Motorcycle Contingent), which in 2006 was able to establish the organization's name as a trademark after convincing the federal government that "dyke" was not a dirty word.

In addition to Dykes on Bikes, parade regulars include the organization Parents, Families and Friends of Lesbians and Gays (PFLAG), as well as supportive politicians and church groups. Furthermore, the parade provides evidence that LGBT people are everywhere. There'll be a contingent of elderly gays and lesbians ("2-4-6-8, how do you know your grandma's straight?"), and a group from Alcoholics Anonymous ("2-4-6-8, we remember who we date"). The parade includes LGBT physicians, LGBT deaf people, cyclists, socialists, American Indians, and a large contingent of LGBT folks from government agencies.

The event has grown in numbers of participants and onlookers from its modest beginnings to crowds in the hundred of thousands. Many of the spectators are tourists, and each year their most common refrain remains, "This is nothing like we'd see back home!"

How?

57. How Does One Celebrate Chinese New Year?

First off, not on January 1. The Chinese New Year is calculated in accordance with the lunar year which normally (but not always) means the event will be designated for celebration in February. Each astrological year is represented by an animal equated with one of the 12 signs of the Chinese zodiac. For instance, 2010 was the year of the Tiger (brave, rash, impetuous, warm, sincere), 2011 was the year of the Rabbit (withdrawn, independent, aloof, submissive, humble) and 2013 the Year of the Snake (calm, shy, cautious, but argumentative). In San Francisco, the celebration of Chinese New Year goes on for a couple of weeks during which time those who celebrate the holiday clean their houses, pay their debts, purchase new clothes and gift their children with money presented in red envelopes.

The celebration climaxes with the Chinese New Year Parade, which, like fortune cookies, is a Chinese-American invention, not a staple on the Asian continent. The parade begins at Second and Market Streets and concludes at Kearny and Columbus. Viewers are treated to performing stilt walkers, lion dancers, Chinese acrobats and, the *pièce de résistance*, the 201-foot-long Golden Dragon with its rainbow-colored pom-poms, colored lights, and white rabbit fur trimming. It takes a team of 100 men and women, honorees of the community, to carry this symbol of strength, adventure, courage, and prosperity. At the conclusion of the event, seemingly in violation of a variety of state and local ordinances, as many as 600,000 firecrackers are set off to—it is thought—scare off evil spirits and entice the gods of wealth to peoples' doorsteps.

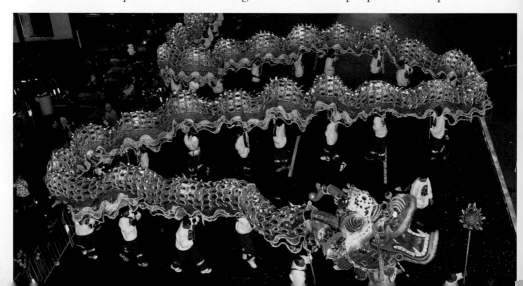

How?

58. How does the Mission District's Cinco de Mayo Celebration Differ from Its Carnaval?

There are big differences between these two festive events, but also similarities in that both are colorful and fun. Cinco de Mayo is not hard to keep in your appointment book. The parade takes place on a weekend day closest to the fifth of May each year, usually beginning at 20th and Mission Streets and concluding at 24th and Potrero Streets. Do not confuse Cinco de Mayo with either Mexican Independence Day (September 16th commemorating the beginning of the 1810 revolt against Spanish rule) or with the official birthday of the Mexican Revolution (November 20th commemorating the overthrow of the dictator Porfirio Diaz in 1910). These important events are also celebrated in San Francisco, but not with the fervor of Cinco de Mayo.

Cinco de Mayo has, in fact, more North American roots than these other celebrations, coming into its own in the 1960s when the United Farm Workers and Cesar Chavez were promoting Chicano identity. The event commemorates the Battle of Puebla, May 5, 1862, when a small poorly-equipped Mexican army defeated the powerful French Napoleonic army. The Mexicans eventually lost to the French, who occupied Mexico for a number of years, but this outcome does not deter from the heroic Mexican spirit exhibited on that day in May.

By contrast, the Mission District's Carnaval is a more eclectic celebration of Latin culture than Cinco de Mayo. Launched in 1979 by a group of Mission District artists, San Francisco's May Carnaval doesn't quite fit the Carnaval tradition. The traditional Carnaval—think Rio—is intended symbolically as the last fling of sensual indulgence before the pre-Easter rollback that is Lent. Unlike Rio's weather, San Francisco's weather in March and April can induce goose bumps, particularly when low temperatures make contact with exposed flesh. Flesh being a *de rigueur* element of Carnaval costumes, the San Francisco celebration moved to the balmier days of May and has become not about Lent, but rather about an international celebration of spring. Front and center at the event are Trinidadians, Bolivians, Brazilians, and Salvadorans and others from South America. But no one is surprised to see also Filipinos, Chinese, Lebanese and Ghanaians. The event has become a kind of UN General Assembly that swings.

What's This?

59. The International Hotel

This mural, celebrating Filipino-American culture, fronts the former International Hotel at Kearny and Jackson Streets. The "I Hotel" to the locals, lives in a very different envelope than it did in the 1970s when, before its demolition, the site became ground zero in the development wars. Now 14 stories of senior housing rise above a ground floor that houses an art gallery and Filipino-American history center.

Between 1979 and 2005 the site was no more than a gaping hole, a reminder of earlier battles. Up until the 1950s, the I-Hotel had been one of many hotels along Kearny between Columbus and Bush Streets that housed almost exclusively Filipino men. Because of exclusionary immigration practices that were anything but family friendly, these men led bachelor lives. Some were migrant farm workers who came to the city during the offseason. Others worked in the city as cooks, waiters, bellhops, house servants, chauffeurs, and elevator operators.

A vibrant cultural ghetto known as Manilatown evolved in the neighborhood. Locals could patronize the New Luneta Café, the Bataan Lunch, Mango's Smoke Shop, Blanco's Bar, and Teno's Barber Shop.

Sheriff Richard Hongisto in front of I-Hotel after Aug. 4, 1977 eviction.

In the mid–1950s, the expanding Financial District was encroaching on Manilatown, and the hotels and community services began to disappear. The I–Hotel was about the last vestige of this vanishing community. In 1968, the owners of the hotel—a consortium of interests headed by San Francisco real estate mogul Walter Shorenstein—served eviction notices on the residents who were, for the most part, *manongs* (male elders in the Filipino community). The developers wanted the property to build a parking garage.

Anyone with a passing understanding of issues like this in San Francisco will have a pretty good idea of what came next. Picket lines went up; legal battle ensued. For activist students from local universities stopping the eviction of the *manongs* became a *cause célèbre*. The residents also had friends in the establishment. Dianne Feinstein (then president of the Board of Supervisors), Mayor George Moscone and Sheriff Richard Hongisto supported the residents' cause.

Shorenstein bailed out, selling the property to the Four Seas Corporation. Like many who had signed on to attack the problem of urban blight during these years, he was a bit mystified by developments. "I thought I was getting rid of a slum," he said.

Finally, in the summer of 1977, Four Seas got the court order to proceed with the eviction. At first, Hongisto, who as sheriff was supposed to act as *majordomo* for the residents' removal, refused to do it. He was sent to jail for five days. But by August 4, he accepted the inevitable. About 1 a.m. on that day, the onslaught began.

Some 1,000 demonstrators, mostly the young and radicalized, showed up, linked arms and confronted the police in front of the hotel. After a struggle, the cops were able to clear the street and then, using Fire Department ladders, entered the building from the roof. Hongisto himself swung a sledgehammer. His words, however, were cajoling: "I'd appreciate it if you would come out; it's time to go." The eviction was over by dawn so as not to interfere with Financial District traffic.

The episode of the International Hotel had cost San Francisco $3 million and a lot of bad national publicity. U.S. Senator Frank Church of the Senate's Committee on Aging sent a delegation to investigate the eviction. Yet there was also an upside to the shameful removal of these old men. A movement had coalesced. The city enacted an ordinance forbidding demolition of residential hotels; voters passed limits on downtown construction; and nutrition, housing and safety programs for the elderly moved closer to reality.

Why Is It Called?

60. Lotta's Fountain

Lotta Crabtree did not need to take out a loan in 1875 when she presented the city she loved with this fountain located at the significant intersection of Market and Kearny Streets. By then, she was the richest actress in America, after embarking on her moneymaking ways at a very young age.

In 1852, as a 6-year-old, arriving in San Francisco with her mother, Lotta brought with her the combination of beauty, charm, and talent that would propel her to success. In a city where there were few children, the always laughing Lotta gleaned much attention in the town that a few years later was to designate her "The San Francisco Favorite."

Lotta's father, who had come to California to mine gold, had, by 1853, settled down to a more prosaic occupation: running a boarding house for the miners in the bustling Sierra foothill town of Grass Valley. He needed his wife and daughter to help out. When the family settled in, it turned out they were living a couple of doors away from the notorious entertainer and courtesan, Lola Montez, who was taking a respite from her former life as mistress to Franz Liszt, Alexander Dumas and King Ludwig of Bavaria. Montez recognized Lotta's budding talent and suggested the girl go with her on a Australian tour as kind of an opening act. But Lotta's mother, Mary Ann, had other ideas. She took her daughter on another type of tour, performing in the mining camps of the Gold Country. Lotta was a natural, dancing the jig and the fandango, playing the horn pipe and the banjo, and energetically belting out the songs of the times. The miners showered the little girl with gold nuggets and coins, which her mother scrupulously stored in a trunk.

Returning to San Francisco in 1856, Lotta continued to charm patrons at theaters, saloons and dance halls, while her mother proceeded to stash the take. If a coin-filled trunk got too heavy to haul around, Mary Ann would invest the contents in real estate. In 1864, when Lotta set out to entertain the wider world, her admirers in San Francisco presented her with a wreath of pure gold.

Lotta had by now taken up acting, and, because of her small stature, often took on children's roles, notably as Little Nell in a stage adaptation of Charles Dickens' *Old Curiosity Shop*. As Lotta's fame and fortune increased so did her philanthropy. That's when she bestowed her fountain on San Francisco. The cast iron piece, said to remind Lotta of a prop from one of her stage plays, provided water fonts for passersby and watering troughs for horses. At the dedication, ev-

eryone seemed happy except a few serious imbibers who, not finding a beer or whiskey spigot, were on the verge of rioting.

Lotta's Fountain soon became a popular meeting place for shoppers and saloon crawlers. With the earthquake and fire of 1906, the meetings at the fountain became more serious. Because it was one of the few structures left standing on Market Street, the fountain served as a gathering spot and message center for earthquake survivors. That's why San Franciscans congregate at the fountain at 5:12 a.m. each April 18 to commemorate the exact moment of the catastrophe. By 1906, Lotta had retired, but her qualities of cheerful optimism and impulsive energy were the same ones that inspired the population of the city she loved, motivating its citizens to rise from the ashes.

Why?

61. Why is Lombard Street Crooked?

Let's start with this: Lombard Street between Hyde and Leavenworth is not—as advertised—the "Crookedest Street in the World," or even the crookedest street in San Francisco. The latter honor belongs to Vermont Street between 20th and 22nd Streets near San Francisco General Hospital. However, both of these Streets are crooked for the same reason: The switchback design on Lombard was conceived in 1922 to accommodate Russian Hill's 27 percent grade. The street builders had recently paved the even steeper Green Street, a few blocks over, and realized they did not need one more street that would provide a perilous challenge for vehicles.

It was Bill Cosby who told a knowing audience at San Francisco's Hungry i in the 1960s why flowers grow along this block of Lombard. They're for "the people who have killed themselves" maneuvering this street, he said. This observation was echoed in 1987 by Board of Supervisors President John Molinari and Russian Hill resident, who wanted the city to close the winding cobblestone street. "We have to stop selling this as some major attraction, because it's just not safe," he said. "It's a magnet for rude tourists who cause traffic jams and accidents." But tourists, rude or not, continue to flock to the street, that is still very much with us.

Lombard Street has starred in movies (*What's Up Doc?, The Love Bug*) and video games (*Grand Theft Auto: San Andreas*) all the while providing visitors with something of a low-grade roller coaster ride.

What's This?

62. San Francisco Armory

I f this building looks ominously foreboding it has accomplished its purpose. It was the arsenal of the California National Guard, erected in all its Moorish splendor at 14th and Mission Streets between 1912 and 1914. A new building was needed because while the guardsmen were deterring looters during the 1906 earthquake and fire, their Western Addition headquarters had burned down.

The early years of the last century were edgy ones with labor and radical unrest on the rise, so it was decided that the Guard, which was charged with confronting such disturbances, should have an impenetrable fortress at the center of town. The 200,000-square-foot building was constructed with 18-inch thick walls. The four octagon towers and narrow, lancet, and rectangular windows did not invite trespassers. On any single occasion, 15,000 guardsmen could go through their paces at the Armory. The guardsmen had an opportunity to try out their skills when the company was called on to suppress the 1934 waterfront strike, a convenient mile or so away. The intervention left two strikers dead and many injured.

The centerpiece of the building is the 39,000-square-foot Drill Court where the guardsmen engaged in close order maneuvers. But the Armory boasted plenty of other features to attract recruits. There was a gymnasium, a swimming pool, an industrial kitchen, a banquet room, and a shooting range in the basement.

During its prime, from the 1920s to the 1940s, the Armory doubled as a sports pavilion, earning the name "Madison Square Garden of the West." For more than 30 years, at least two prizefights a week were held in the Drill Court, some featuring welter- and light heavyweight champions.

However, as a site for military maneuvers, the Armory has been used only sparingly, most notably during the mobilization for the Korean War in the early 1950s. By the late '50s, close order drill was no longer a central part of the National Guard regimen. By 1976, the building had been vacated by the Guard, though two years later it was added to the National Register of Historic Places. As the building now seemed here to stay, the site went through a number of uses and proposed uses. Scenes from *Star Wars* movies were filmed here; the San Francisco Opera used the site to construct sets and hold rehearsals. There were plans to use the space for storage lockers, a rehabilitation clinic, a rock climbing

gymnasium, a dot-com office park, and a telecommunication switching center. There were suggestions for high-end housing and for affordable housing. None of this seemed to fly. The Armory was "a herd of white elephants," according to one critic.

But in 2006, Kink.com, a San Francisco-based internet pornography company specializing in bondage and fetish videos, bought the building for $14.5 million to use as a production center. There was the predictable neighborhood concern: a nearby school, etc. As it turns out, the company has been a pretty good neighbor and an excellent steward of the building. The 160 rooms certainly fit the company's needs: one room is decked out as a 1930s speakeasy, another in Victorian splendor, another as a dungeon with copious hardware, and on and on. All with the latest technology.

One reminder of the building's origins remains. In the basement, one can see the remnants of Mission Creek, one of those underground sources of water that once flowed freely through the neighborhood. It's because of the creek that the Armory is located where it is. In case of a siege, the authorities did not want the troops to go thirsty.

Who Thought of . . . ?

63. Levi's

You might reasonably conjecture that someone named Levi thought of Levi's. But the answer is a little trickier. Levi Strauss, did not invent Levi's. Rather the honor belongs to a Reno, Nevada, tailor by the name of Jacob Davis. However, if it weren't for Levi Strauss we would not likely have the durable trousers that have been part of our haberdashery landscape for generations.

Here's how events that led to San Francisco's Levi's empire transpired. In 1847, at age 18, Levi Strauss emigrated to the United States from Bavaria. Settling in Louisville, Kentucky, he scraped out a living as an itinerant peddler, toting 100 pounds of sewing materials, blankets, and kettles. When news of the California Gold Rush of 1849 reached the East Coast, Levi Strauss saw an alternative to selling pots and pans. In 1853 he took a ship to San Francisco. He did not head for the gold fields, which were quickly depleting. Instead, he set up a San Francisco dry goods shop. In a city of not much more than 50,000, there were already 117 dry goods stores. However, Levi Strauss had an advantage. Many of the stores were perennially understocked, and Levi had brothers in the dry goods business in New York City who made sure his San Francisco enterprise was amply supplied. Successful by 1866, Levi Strauss was able to move his headquarters to Battery Street, not far from the current Levi's Plaza, where he installed such cutting-edge accoutrements as gaslights and a freight elevator.

Levi Strauss's big break came in 1873 when one of his clients, Nevada tailor Jacob Davis, contacted him. Davis had been buying heavy cotton from Strauss to fashion into trousers for some while. But there was a problem. Subjected to the rigors of life in the mining camps, the pockets of these pants would rip beyond repair. Of course, a pocket decimated is a useless pocket. Davis's customers complained constantly. In an act of creative semi-desperation, he placed rivets on the corners of the pockets. Problem solved, and Davis had the prototype that was to become Levi's as we know them. Lacking the business acumen and the $81 necessary to file a patent, Davis approached Levi Strauss for the fee, offering to share the patent. Strauss knew a good deal when he saw it. He brought Davis to San Francisco to manage production. Soon thousands in the city were wearing "Levi's"—which became the company's registered trademark—and before long the company was employing many hundreds. By 1886, Strauss left the day-today work at the company, devoting much of his time to philanthropic endeavors, including endowments to the University of California.

Strauss died in 1902 at age 72. He was unmarried and had no children. The firm passed to his four nephews whose descendents still own and manage the company. The firm's slogan at the turn of the last century had been "For men who toil." These catchwords do not seem to have lost their relevance. But now the toilers are often men and women packing laptops, not pitchforks.

501 Jeans, c. 1890

What's This?

64. The Barbary Coast Hippodrome

This exterior at 555 Pacific Avenue is the most tantalizing remnant of a neighborhood that was once known for its dizzying excess. Now home to an art supply store, this location once housed the Hippodrome, one of the more than 500 saloons, dance halls, and whorehouses packed cheek to jowl along and around Pacific in the years before and after the 1906 earthquake and fire. Labeled the Barbary Coast after the equally unsafe pirate-infested region off the coast of Africa, from 1860 on, the neighborhood was as enticing to many as it was dangerous.

Writing in 1876, Benjamin Estelle Lloyd described it as a "hell, of dance halls and saloons where bleary-eyed men and women do everything to heap upon themselves degradation. Licentiousness, debauchery, pollution, loathsome disease, insanity from dissipation, misery, poverty, wealth, profanity, blasphemy, and death are all there." Despite this repulsive catalogue, or perhaps because of it, the Barbary Coast ranked high on the list of attractions for natives and tourists.

Prostitution was the neighborhood's major industry. Here the low-end establishments housed "cribs," small rooms of about 4-feet-by-8-feet. As many as 300 women, often overseen by nasty pimps, plied their trade in such places.

By contrast, the Hippodrome, a dance palace with artsy bas-relief panels depicting satyrs in lecherous pursuit of nymphs, was rather at the high end of the degeneracy spectrum. Nevertheless, for male patrons, it was a case of buyer beware. A woman skilled in the art of removing cash from her dance partner's pockets could significantly supplement her base pay, often ignoring the house rule to share the take with the club owner. The girls would further manipulate the drunk and in-heat customer with the old key trick, saying "I want you to come to my place afterwards, a few dollars will get you the key." Of course, it was the wrong key and the wrong address. The police cracked down on this practice when numerous homeowners complained about drunken men searching fruitlessly in the middle of the night for locks their keys would not open.

In 1913, responding to the editorial nudging of William Randolph Hearst of the *San Francisco Examiner,* the city issued a death knell of regulations to the Barbary Coast's good and not so good times: no dancing in saloons and no woman employees or patrons allowed in these establishments. The owner of the Hippodrome suggested separate sections for ladies and for gentlemen, but an at-

USE OTHER DOOR→

tempt to separate the sexes in such a libidinous environment seemed naive, if not disingenuous. The idea was rejected by both patrons and the city fathers.

The Hippodrome did manage to hold on for a number of years as a more or less legitimate nightclub, and was conscripted into a movie performance as Ned Galvin's nightclub in the 1957 film *Pal Joey*. It's here that Frank Sinatra meets up with both Rita Hayworth and Kim Novak. The former clients of the Hippodrome could only have dreamed of such luck.

Who Thought of . . . ?

65. San Francisco Topless Dancing

Here's the Condor Club, still in existence at Columbus and Broadway Streets, though now somewhat subdued from its *la dolce vita* beginnings. It is here that "Big Davey" Rosenberg invented San Francisco-style topless dancing. Weighing in at 400-plus pounds, Rosenberg was once described as "a belly closely followed by a man." He called himself "the world's greatest press agent," a claim the *Los Angeles Times* acknowledged, "because of his bulk, few would quibble with."

In 1964, Rosenberg was employed as a publicist for the Condor. This club and others in North Beach were doing a middling business by featuring caged young women in bikinis dancing "the Swim," "the Frug," and "the Watusi." That was before June 19, when Rosenberg saw a Joseph Magnin Company newspaper ad for the monokini by the designer Rudi Gernreich. The monokini, a bikini without the top, had caused something of a stir when introduced in Paris. It was said that, unable to hire models to wear his product, Gernreich recruited prostitutes.

Seeing the ad, Rosenberg beelined to Magnin's and bought a $25 monokini. Returning to the club, he presented the garment to cocktail waitress/go-go dancer Carol Doda. Later that night, Doda made the most of her entrance, descending , bare-breasted, from the ceiling atop a grand piano. Mesmerized, patrons recognized this was a first.

News of the breast baring spread rapidly, aided by the fact that delegates from the Republican National Convention were in town looking for diversion. Soon there were topless clubs all around North Beach, at one-time as many as 28. Doda was performing 12 shows a night. Within months, the craze went national. There were topless restaurants, topless girl bands, topless shoeshine parlors and topless ice cream stands.

Recognizing that more is more, Doda underwent silicone breast injections. What had been a proportional 36-inch bosom now expanded to an eye-popping 44 inches. Rosenberg made sure the mammary enhancements were insured by Lloyd's of London for $1.5 million.

The Condor installed a 40-foot sign out front featuring a neon and nude version of Doda with blinking nipples.

All this got the attention of city fathers. One supervisor wanted the Broad-

way clubs exposed as hangouts for "punks, muggers, cutthroats and molesters." The police chief responded that there were many fewer muggers and molesters in North Beach than in some other neighborhoods, Not mollified, Mayor John Shelley insisted, "Topless is at the bottom of it all." Eventually, in April 1965, there was a police raid, rumored to have been provoked by a phone call from publicist Rosenberg. There was a trial, but the judge found that a bared breast as entertainment fell well within the boundaries of acceptable community standards.

By the '70s, however, topless was pretty much old hat. In the 1980s, the neon nipples quit flashing and someone provided the Doda caricature with a dance hall skirt. In 1991, the sign came down. There was a campaign to donate it to the Smithsonian Museum in Washington, D.C. The museum director politely declined, saying the institution did not have room. Supporters of the sign weren't so sure. As one admirer of the ribald topless era put it: "If they can find room for the *Enola Gay* they should be able to find room for Carol Doda."

Who's This?

66. George Moscone

This is sculptor Robert Arneson's aw-shucks depiction of George Moscone, who served as San Francisco's mayor from 1975 until 1978, the year he was gunned down, along with San Francisco Supervisor Harvey Milk, by Dan White—a former supervisor. After White had abruptly resigned his office, he decided he wanted his job back. Moscone refused to reappoint him. That decision was enough to lead White on the shooting rampage that brought down White and Moscone.

Arneson, who had been commissioned to do a memorial piece for the convention center that would bear Moscone's name, was not into monumental and celebratory sculpture. Rather he had established his reputation since the 1960s as the leading West Coast artist of pieces executed in ceramic that were colorful, quirky, and whimsical. He might create in ceramic a typewriter or a self-portrait of himself as a chef or hipster. His pieces were non-conformist and irreverent. Maybe he wasn't the best choice to produce a piece celebrating the martyred mayor.

When Arneson delivered the piece no one seemed to mind the bust's cartoonish quality. That dimension, in fact, reflected the former mayor's ebullient personality. The problem was with the pedestal on which the head had been placed. Arneson had decided to create a graffiti-like biography on the base of the work calling attention to events in Moscone's life and career. Some of his scrawlings referred to milestones in the former mayor's biography such as, "Hastings Law School," Moscone's law school alma mater. Others picked up on his commonly used phrases, including, "Trust me on this one." Still others referred to the dark events of the Moscone/Milk murders: "Smith and Wesson"—the weapon that Dan White had used to commit his crime—images of bloodstained bullets, and the words, "BANG BANG BANG BANG BANG." The San Francisco Arts Commission had ordered the work and was getting worried. In deference to George Moscone's widow, Gina, it was kept veiled on the day the Moscone Center was to be dedicated. Emotions concerning the killings were still running raw, and, adding to the prevailing gloom, only a week before the dedication more than 900 Bay Area residents had committed mass suicide in Guyana at the behest of their leader the Rev. Jim Jones.

Among those particularly upset by the Arneson work was Mayor Dianne Feinstein, who, as president of the Board of Supervisors, had assumed the mayor's

duties when Moscone died. She asked Arneson to alter the pedestal; he refused, saying the disputed inscriptions were integral to the work. Feinstein then lobbied the Arts Commission to reject the piece. They did, and it was returned to Arneson, who returned his commission and sold the work to a collector for $50,000.

In 2012, the San Francisco Museum of Modern Art acquired the work, which retains the affectionate title *Portrait of George*. Said Neal Benezra the museum director, "It's always struck me as an incredibly powerful work." "Iconic," he called it.

67. How Do You Get a Street Named After You in San Francisco?

T hese days, as one might guess, there is no end to the rigmarole that must be navigated to accomplish this feat. In the early days it was easier:

1. Get elected president before 1880: Washington, Jackson, Fillmore, and others, but not Buchanan. Contrary to popular belief, President James Buchanan was beat out in the name game by another Buchanan, one John Buchanan, an auctioneer who had sold many San Francisco lots. The street was named after the latter Buchanan in 1856. James Buchanan did not become president until 1857.

2. Be on board at the beginning: Even though before 1849 only about 300 brave souls had committed to life in San Francisco (then Yerba Buena), the most prominent of these men were in the right place at the right time to have a street named after them or maybe to name a street after themselves. Check out Howard, Brannan, Bryant, Larkin, Leidesdorff, Davis, and Richardson—all among the pioneer settlers.

3. Take up surveying: O'Farrell Street is named for the surveyor Jasper O'Farrell, who greatly irritated some property owners in 1845 by proposing the diagonal gash that is Market Street, thus playing havoc with property rights along the route. A few years later his reputation had recovered to the point where he had a street named after him. O'Farrell brought others along with him. No one knows for sure the person that Bush Street honors. But the most credible conjecture points to one J. B. Bush, a cabin boy on a ship who deserted once he hit San Francisco. He went to work for O'Farrell, and was rewarded with a street name, perhaps the youngest San Franciscan so honored. After O'Farrell came surveyor William Eddy and voilà!—Eddy Street.

4. Get yourself named to a street naming committee: Charles Gough was a San Francisco milkman in 1850, who spent his days riding through the city's outer reaches with two milk cans strapped to his saddle. After many years in this service, he was appointed in 1885 to a committee to lay out and name the Streets of the Western Addition. So ever after we have had a Gough Street, an Octavia—named for Gough's sister—and a Steiner Street— named for Gough's good friend who delivered water in the area.

Who Thought of . . . ?

68. Steam Beer

The folks at Anchor Steam Beer, the company that now owns the "steam beer" trademark, pinpoint the brewer who created this invigorating quaff. The honor belongs to Gottlieb Brekle, who came to California with his family in 1849. Brekle, like other sharp business types, arrived not to pan gold, but to make money off of those who did. His niche was going to make use of his expertise as a producer of lager beer.

But that wasn't so easy. Lager requires cold fermentation and in the temperate climate of California there was no cold stuff to do the job. Sure, the Sierra Nevada had plenty of ice, but in the days before refrigeration there was no way to transport this ingredient to the warmer climes. Brekle was not to be diverted. He let his lager yeast ferment at lower temperatures, adding some additional hops to prevent spoilage. The result was steam beer: not quite a lager, not quite an ale.

As to where the appellation steam beer comes from, the explanation is up for grabs. It could derive from the hissing sound that the beer makes during the heated fermentation process or the spraying sound that one hears as a new barrel is tapped, or maybe the steam that rose from the brewery as the beverage cooled.

At any rate, it should be said that steam beer did not always possess the sophisticated "Only in San Francisco" cache associated with it today. "Not a connoisseur's drink," noted the *Western Brewer* magazine in 1893. In his 1891 novel, *McTeague*, set in San Francisco, Frank Norris has the doomed McTeague devote his free time to swilling steam beer, a pretty lowlife habit in Norris's eyes.

The resurrection of steam beer to its iconic status has a lot to do with the obsession of one man, Fritz Maytag of Maytag washing machines. In 1965, Maytag was drinking at the Old Spaghetti Factory in North Beach, then one of the few remaining purveyors of Anchor Steam Beer, when he learned that the brewery would be closing in one week. He proceeded to buy 51 percent of the stock and spent years refining his product while keeping alive Gottlieb Brekle's basic technique. With the modern-day version of Anchor Steam, the turn-of-the-century imbiber like McTeague would be in for a whole new taste experience.

Why Is It Called . . . ?

69. Woodward's Garden

Located at 1700 Mission Street below a tangle of a freeway overpasses, this inauspicious and well-established restaurant draws its name—Woodward's Garden—from the 1866 pleasure palace that once occupied this same terrain, Robert Woodward's mansion and its environs, bordered by Mission, 13th, Valencia, and 15th Streets. Woodward, the Forty-Niner, understood that more money was to be made off the miners than in the gold mines. He opened a grocery store and then a thriving hotel and restaurant—the What Cheer House on Sacramento Street—acquiring a fortune from these and other investments. As was *de rigueur* among the newly rich, Woodward promptly built a very big home. But that was just the start of his indulgence. His real interest was in creating a great garden and collecting anything he could get his hands on.

Ever the entrepreneur, as more and more people came to gape at the four-acre premises, Woodward decided to move his family to the Napa Valley and open the gates to visitors for a fee. The mansion became the Museum of Natural Wonders filled with stuffed birds and bears, fossils, antique relics, and a 97-pound gold nugget from a Sierra Butte mine. There was a gallery full of copies of the works of the old masters of Europe and kids' rides, including a rotary boat that whirled around a circular track on the edge of a pond, a curiosity and delight in a town still getting used to children.

The gardens were a maze of gravel paths that passed fountains, streams, small lakes and hills, man-made grottoes, and caverns. Trees and shrubs were imported from Europe. Ostriches, deer, and barnyard animals wandered the grounds that housed the largest zoo on the West Coast and an amphitheatre where up to 5,000 spectators could watch fire eaters, Japanese acrobats, dancing bears, and Roman chariot races.

Until Robert Woodward's death in 1879, the gardens remained San Francisco's premier recreation location. Then, inevitably, the property began to deteriorate. The collections were sold off, many items resurfacing at Sutro Baths. The hilly acres were leveled and sold to developers, who built tracts of homes for the city's burgeoning working class.

WOODWARD'S GARDENS·1875

What Are These?

70. Mary Ellen Pleasant's Trees

These eucalyptus trees on the west side of Octavia Street at Bush provide only a wispy remembrance of the mansion that once occupied an entire block at this site. The palatial residence, with its 30 rooms, sweeping entrance, Corinthian columns, and spectacular Mansard roof, was home to Mary Ellen Pleasant, known locally as "Mammy" Pleasant. "Mammy" was something of a pejorative epithet, laid on her by local newspapers because Pleasant was a black woman. But her regal bearing and multimillion-dollar net worth did little to support this *Stepin Fetchit* stereotype.

Born a slave around 1814, her biography has been distorted and obscured by misinformation. Her chroniclers have mixed truth, exaggeration, and falsehood to cast her in many roles: housekeeper, financier, abolitionist, hypnotist, abortionist, thief, master chef, matchmaker, blackmailer, madam, charlatan, benefactor, and murderer.

Here is some of what we do know. An octoroon freed from slavery by a sympathetic owner, she served years as an indentured servant in New England, developing extraordinary business and culinary skills. Marrying in the 1840s, she became a slave rescuer, aiding escapees to reach the North. When, in the 1850s, she herself found she was pursued by bounty hunters, she left the South for points west, arriving in San Francisco in 1852. The city, with a population of 50,000, many men to every woman, and 700 drinking and gambling establishments, presented exactly the kind of milieu that a clever and ambitious transplant such as Pleasant could take advantage of.

She used the inheritance of her now deceased husband to parlay profits from hospitality ventures to investments in laundries, real estate, stocks and mining. She got to know the city's movers and shakers, scheming to get the goods on everyone who was anyone. She did this by drawing on the contacts from her previous life, bringing to San Francisco women who had escaped slavery and placing them as servants in the homes of San Francisco upper crust. At these locations the women were privy to the dirty laundry (literally and figuratively) of the monied classes. This intelligence they happily shared with Pleasant. That's where the blackmailing accusations came from.

But Pleasant's dog-eat-dog capitalist instincts are only part of her story. During her California years, she was a dedicated advocate for the cause of blacks. She fought to keep fugitive slaves from being returned to bondage. She

funded John Brown's slave-freeing attempt at Harper's Ferry. In 1868, many decades before Rosa Parks, Pleasant sued and won the right for African Americans to ride San Francisco's trolleys. She was also active in the campaign that gave blacks the right to serve on California juries.

In the end, however, Pleasant's greatest good fortune contributed to her downfall. On her journey to California she had met one Thomas Bell, who was to rise to be a director in the powerful Bank of California. Bell and Pleasant became business partners and, some say, secret lovers at a time when black-white unions were forbidden. Successful together in business, when Pleasant built the Octavia Street showpiece, Bell moved in. Pleasant soon arranged a wife for Bell. This eyebrow-raising arrangement caused tongues to wag. There were melodramatic tales of voodoo rites and wild orgies. In 1892, when Bell fell to his death from a landing at the mansion, Pleasant was suspected, then cleared of involvement. A few years later, Bell's wife went on the attack, circulating over-the-top stories in the press about what she claimed were Pleasant's bizarre carryings-on. Pleasant was forced from the house, and died close to broke in 1904, still living under the cloud of unsubstantiated smears.

Mary Ellen Pleasant at age 87 as she appeared in her 1902 autobiography.

Who's This?

71. Sun Yat-sen

This is China's first president, Dr. Sun Yat-sen, the prime mover in the 1911 overthrow of that country's 300-year-old Manchu Dynasty. He stands here in the relatively peaceful Financial District enclave of St. Mary's Square. San Francisco's favorite sculptor, Beniamino "Benny" Bufano, created this 14-foot-high, red granite and stainless-steel sculpture whose tranquility matches the environment.

Bufano was an admirer of Dr. Sun whom he met during his travels in China. Here the artist learned from porcelain glazers the techniques he put to use in many of his works, including this one.

The statue was commissioned in 1938, 13 years after Sun's death, by Chinatown leaders as a recognition of Sun's travels to San Francisco. In the early years of the last century, he had come to the city seven times, sometimes hiding out from agents of the Chinese government out to kill him, but mostly to raise funds to finance his revolution. In that regard he succeeded dramatically, raising from the American Chinese community upward of $400,000, a princely sum back then. Often standing at the very spot where his likeness is now portrayed, Sun addressed the local population on the guiding principles of the emerging Chinese republic. He told the American Chinese they could support his cause by raising money through peddling Chinese goods to tourists, a tradition still firmly entrenched.

When the revolution occurred, Sun became president of the new republic, but only for six weeks before he was deposed. However, this was time enough for him to ban the practice of footbinding and for many of his American followers to celebrate his victory by cutting off their once obligatory queues.

Though his tenure as president was short, the Kuomintang, the nationalist party which he founded, lived on and is established as the principal party of Taiwan where it founded a rival government to the People's Republic of China.

However, Sun is no less a hero to mainland Chinese where the party line *People's Daily* newspaper has called him a "great revolutionary, who fought against imperialism and for the freedom of China."

Sun held convictions that seemed to elevate him above the squabbles of day-to-day politics. This point of view is evidenced by his words engraved in

Chinese on another San Francisco landmark—the Gate at Grant Avenue and Bush Street, which marks the entrance to Chinatown. It reads: "All under heaven is for food of the people."

Why Is This There?

72. Treasure Island

This 400-acre man-made island at the center of San Francisco Bay was built to celebrate great events. In the mid-1930s, the country was still mired in the despair of the Great Depression. But by the end of the decade two engineering and aesthetic marvels, the Golden Gate Bridge and the San Francisco-Oakland Bay Bridge, would thread their way across San Francisco Bay, brightening the spirit of the locals. It was time for an international exposition.

Two previous San Francisco international expositions—the California International Midwinter Exposition of 1894 and the Panama Pacific Exposition of 1915—had been off-the-charts successes. This one would glorify the technological accomplishments of the bay-spanning bridges. But where would this event take place? There was only one location where both the honored structures would be in full view, and that was at the heart of San Francisco Bay.

So in 1936, with funding from the federal government, workers began dredging 29 million yards of mud and fill from the bottom of the bay and depositing it on the shoals of Yerba Buena Island to create the largest man-made island ever.

When the Golden Gate International Exposition opened in 1939 it presented visitors with an architectural mélange never seen before or since. Many of San Francisco's premier architects were employed to design buildings collectively labeled the "Pacifica Style." The future—the exposition designers implied—was the Pacific Rim. The buildings hinted of Latin America and South Asia. Mixed with art deco structures were pyramids, elephant heads, and pilasters meant to imitate those of Angkor Wat. Rare tropical species of orchids, hibiscus, and datura were imported to enhance the exotic atmosphere.

But most of the exposition's attractions were still American enough. Benny Goodman played for swing dancers, Jack Benny told jokes, and Sally Rand teased with her skin-exposing fan dance at her Nude Ranch. Visitors to the fair were to see their first robot, atom smasher, television projection, and electric dishwasher.

A gigantic cash register from the National Cash Register Co. rang up daily attendance. Unfortunately, the numbers were disappointing. Maybe no one anticipated the winds that reached such levels that the clarion bells atop

the exposition's center piece, the Tower of the Sun, could be heard in Berkeley. However, the primary reason for the declining attendance was the shadow of Adolf Hitler's war enveloping Europe by 1940. Hitler's ally, Italy, closed its pavilion that year, and the bust of Italian dictator Benito Mussolini was shrouded so no one would see it being carried out.

At the end of the expo, the plan for the island was to convert it into San Francisco's international airport. Once the war intervened, the Navy needed Treasure Island's strategic position in the middle of the bay. By way of a trade, the government offered Mills Field, near Millbrae, and that's where our international airport is today.

Treasure Island under construction, 1938.

Why?

73. Why Are There Parrots on Telegraph Hill?

Short answer: because they didn't like the place they were living previously. We aren't talking here about the coastal regions of Peru and Ecuador where they originally made their homes. Rather these Cherry-headed Conures, as they are more correctly designated, couldn't stand being cooped up in the pet stores where they were being confined in the late 1980s before the imported bird ban of 1993. They not only looked for every chance to escape, they made their unhappiness known through ear-splitting squawks that made them not the cutesy pets that lovers of caged birds had bargained for, a fact that advocated for their release.

The flock, which now numbers more than 200, started small in 1980 with the mating of a monogamous pair. (Monogamy is typical of these birds.) Supposedly the new arrivals flocked to Telegraph Hill. Even though the film and book *The Wild Parrots of Telegraph Hill* have made the parrots stars, Telegraph Hill is not always the best place in the city to find these beautiful creatures. Realistically, they go where the food is: fruit, flowers, leaves, and shoots. They are on the lookout for juniper berries, pine nuts, loquats, and eucalyptus. That quest will take them to the top of Telegraph Hill near Coit Tower, to Sue Bierman Park across from the Ferry Building, as well as to the Presidio and along Dolores Street in the Mission District. In recent years, they have discovered the juniper trees in Brisbane. Unlike the jets that had for years roared over that community 24/7, the parrots do not scream at night.

As this is San Francisco, you can always find someone against anything—even a parrot. There are people who argue that the parrots are encroaching on the ecological territory of the local birds. Mark Bittner, the author of *"Wild Parrots"* and for years a protector and advocate for the birds, disagrees.

> The parrots, along with most of the birds I see here, are living in an artificial environment of planted gardens. The gardens consist of plant species that come from all over the world. Far from being an annoyance, the parrots are an inspiration . . . I see them as personable, humorous and intelligent ambassadors of nature. They are no different from most living beings in that they cherish liberty and fear death. Besides, we brought them here against their will. I figure we owe it to them.

Why?

74. Why Are San Francisco Summers So Cold and Foggy?

« I n the summer," wrote *San Francisco Chronicle* columnist Herb Caen, "San Francisco is like living inside a great gray pearl." Goose-bumped visitors may wax less poetic about our summer fog. Unfortunately, there's not a lot we can do about it. (Someone did try in 1938, when the fog—described as "aviation's greatest peril"—was targeted off the Cliff House by a bomb filled with a supposedly fog-destroying chemical compound. It didn't work. Score one for Mother Nature.)

Ironically, San Francisco summers are cold because it's so hot—inland. In the Central Valley, on the other side of the Coast Range Mountains from San Francisco, summer temperatures are often recorded at 100 degrees and above. These temperatures create hot air which rises, leaving a low-pressure area at the lower altitudes. This circumstance presents an opening for the cool sea air to be sucked landward. This sea air, heavy with water, cools as it rises along the coastal hills. The air condenses, dropping visible vapor. That's fog. The coastal hills act as a barrier protecting—if that's the word—the inland areas from the cooling onslaught of fog. Thanks to our fabled Golden Gate, San Francisco gets special treatment. Fog is funneled through this gap, the opening embracing our little peninsula not in just fog, but, as it is known here, *The Fog*.

Why Is This There?

75. The Cross at the Peak of Mount Davidson

Mount Davidson, located south of Twin Peaks and Portola Boulevard, is, at 935 feet, the highest point in the city. The public land at its peak is near the geographical center of San Francisco. So in 1934, this locale seemed to Italian-Catholic Mayor Angelo Rossi and other city fathers an ideal place to erect a 103-foot concrete cross. The cross would, according to Madie Brown, one of its leading proponents, "Bring light into many a darkened home," during those Depression plagued years, and perhaps "instill the principles of the Golden Rule into American business." George Kelham, one of the city's leading architects, was commissioned to design the structure. On Easter day, 1934, President Franklin Roosevelt pressed a gold telegraph key in Washington, D.C., which activated an electrical signal to floodlights at the monument. For many decades that followed, regular Easter services were held at the base of the cross.

In the 1990s, a group of organizations including the American Civil Liberties Union, the American Jewish Congress, and the Americans United for Separation of Church and State, concluded that this imposing Christian edifice had no constitutional right to public land. A long legal battle ensued before the city came up with a solution. It would auction off to a private entity the 0.38 acres at the top of the hill where the cross was located. The winning bid of $26,000 was submitted by the Council of Armenian-American Organizations of Northern California. The cross is maintained today as a memorial of the 1915 Armenian genocide. Those so inclined are at liberty on Easter Sunday to trudge to this small plot and worship freely.

Who Thought of . . . ?

76. The Martini

In the post-Gold Rush culture of San Francisco, where 743 citizens worked as bartenders in a city of 50,000, it is not surprising that one of them, a fellow named Jerry Thomas, would distinguish himself with a valuable contribution to mixology. The year was 1863, the place: the inviting bar of the Occidental Hotel. On an otherwise ordinary day, Thomas, in a creative mood, served a customer about to embark by ferryboat to the bayside city of Martinez. He told the man, "Here's a new drink I concocted for your trip. We'll call it the Martinez." Over the years, it became clear that "Martinez" did not trip lightly off a drink-sodden tongue, and the name of the drink became "The Martini." The rest is history.

In Martinez, however, they tell a different and contradictory story. This time the imbiber was at a bar in Martinez where the bartender served the man, soon to depart by ferry for San Francisco, with his just invented concoction, "The Martinez Special." The fellow liked it so much he called for a round for the house. Arriving in the city the man entered a saloon and ordered a Martinez, which the bartender, of course, had never heard of. Following the fellow's directions, he proceeded to construct the drink that was to become a staple of bartender's guides ever since.

Whichever version of this account one accepts, if either, we do know that the libation proffered that day—half gin, half dry vermouth, accompanied by dashes of bitters and maraschino syrup—was significantly different from the contemporary poison. The late publican Ed Moose explained the evolution to the modern version: Three press agents, who drank at the Biltmore Hotel in Los Angeles, kept complaining that the barman's martinis were too sweet. Irritated, the bartender cut way back on the vermouth, and thus evolved today's mixture, about eight parts gin to one part vermouth. Now, that's the rule of thumb—until it changes.

Why Is It called . . . ?

77. Tadich Grill
The Original Cold Day Restaurant

The "Tadich" part of the name of this venerable San Francisco restaurant, located since 1968 at 240 California Street, is not difficult to get a handle on. From 1887 to 1928, the restaurant was owned by John Tadich, one of the Croatians from the Dalmatian coast who had run the establishment since 1849 when it served miners as the New World Coffee Saloon, which was at first a glorified tent on what is now Commercial Street. Over the years, the premises became a hangout for high-rolling Republican politicos.

One of these men was Alexander Badlam, the city's assessor. Badlam was the nephew of Sam Brannan, San Francisco's first millionaire. Badlam carried around with him the arrogance of his class. In 1882, up for reelection as assessor and making the rounds of the saloons, he proclaimed loudly, "It's a cold day when I get left," (as in "It'll be a cold day in hell when I won't win the election"). Apparently egotism and overconfidence did not play as well with the voters of the 1880s as they seem to today. When word of Badlam's posturing got out, voters rewarded him with a landslide defeat.

Adding insult to injury, pranksters showed up at his residence with huge slabs of ice that they deposited on his doorstep. Meanwhile, Badlam retreated to the New World Coffee Saloon to nurse his wounds and drown his sorrows.

The owners of the establishment, drawing on instincts that would make a modern vice president for public relations proud, decided to rename their establishment The Cold Day Restaurant.

In 1887, when Tadich became sole owner of the restaurant, he gave Tadich Grill top billing but retained the moniker that had called special attention to the premises. It became The Original Cold Day Restaurant, which it remains today.

Why Is It Called . . . ?

78. The Tenderloin

The Tenderloin, loosely bounded by Market Street on the south, Geary Street on the north, Van Ness Avenue on the west and Powell Street on the east, is the traditionally seedy area nestled next to some of the city's most high-end commercial real estate. It's been "the Tenderloin" since early in the 20th century, when players of every stripe came to reside in small hotels and studio apartments. The gambling dens, billiard parlors, and speakeasies of those years created a background for a world of characters familiar to readers of Dashiell Hammett's San Francisco writings.

As to the appellation "Tenderloin," you have your choice of a few, perhaps apocryphal explanations.

1. The cops were paid extra to work this rough territory; hence they could afford better cuts of meat.

2. The cops were paid off by owners of illicit establishments; so they could afford better cuts of meat.

3. The name is a titillating reference to the body parts of the prostitutes who plied their trade in the area.

4. Less colorfully, the neighborhood may be named for a demographically similar area of New York City.

In recent years, the neighborhood has undergone significant changes. On the one hand, it's less about horseplayers and more about mainliners. On the other, the Tenderloin has been repopulated by Southeast Asian families, particularly Vietnamese. New high-tech businesses are encroaching on these blocks and animal rights activist lobby for an alternative to the "meat is murder" connotation that the term "Tenderloin" suggests.

Who's This?

79. William Ralston

This is William Ralston, here honored with a marker on the Marina Green near the point where he met his demise. Known as the West's Lorenzo de Medici, Ralston was the former Mississippi riverboat pilot who, up until his empire collapsed just before his death, had made fortunes in enterprises as diverse as shipyards, banking, hydraulic mining, currency speculation, and real estate.

He had his active hands in many civic projects, including the development of Golden Gate Park, but none more so than the Palace Hotel, his personal Field of Dreams, completed in 1875. In 1870, in a city of only 150,000 inhabitants, Ralston ordered construction of an 800-room hotel—one room for every 187 residents—which would rival in luxury any hotel in the world.

Ralston spent big. He purchased an entire oak forest in Northern California to provide timber to be used in the hotel's construction. He cajoled the eastern furniture company W. & J. Sloane to come west for the sole purposed of furnishing his hotel. The Palace had 7,000 windows, the first hydraulic elevators in the west (called lifting rooms), an intercom system in every room and a bar now staffed by 30. Guests entered the hotel through a sumptuous carriage entrance, the site of the hotel's Garden Court.

But Ralston wasn't around to see his hotel open. He had always played fast and loose with a buck; it is said he never asked his suppliers how much anything cost.

As the founder and president of the Bank of California, he was as careless with other people's money as he was with his own, siphoning off funds from various enterprises to construct his marvel of a hostelry. On August 26, 1875, two months before the completion of the hotel, the Bank of California collapsed. The next day, Ralston went for his daily swim in San Francisco Bay and drowned. Although he was seen flailing about in the water before he went under, the fact that he was an excellent swimmer whose financial world had disintegrated the day before caused many to have strong suspicions that he had done himself in. Some 50,000 residents joined his funeral cortège. One of his business partners viewed the corpse and said, "It's the best thing he could have done." The man may have had a point, as, after the collapse of his enterprises, many of his associates went to jail.

The Palace itself was pretty much wiped out by the earthquake and fire of 1906.

By 1909, it had been rebuilt to stand tall as the elegant structure it remains.

What Happened to…?

80. The Sutro Baths

It may not be the Parthenon by moonlight, but it's the closest thing we have to genuine ruins within San Francisco's city limits. Today, particularly at night, the site of the former Sutro Baths offers an eerie vista, a crumbling concrete labyrinth encroached on by crashing waves and punctuated by sprouting wild lilies and probing cypress trees. At the beginning of the 20th century, the baths, the world's largest indoor public bathing facility, provided visitors with an experience like no other. This great spa was made possible through the generosity of Adolph Sutro, who had struck it rich in the Comstock Lode silver rush that erupted around Virginia City, Nevada, in the 1860s. The site is as it is today because in 1966, scheduled for demolition, the long-abandoned facility burned mysteriously to the ground.

Sutro opened the baths to the public in 1896. He held to the firm belief that bathing in a country where only one in six families had a bathtub, and most folks that did relegated the experience to a Saturday night ritual, was a healthful activity that needed to be encouraged. In chilly San Francisco, where practically no one went swimming, Sutro provided citizens with six saltwater pools and one freshwater pool. The pools varied in temperature from very chilly to 80 degrees. There were diving platforms, water slides, trampolines, toboggans, and trapeze-like rings that allowed visitors to swing over the water. Bathers making use of the 500 dressing rooms were required to wear standard-issue woolen suits with gray white stripes. After all, this was not intended to be the beach at Ipanema. Some 25,000 people could revel at Sutro Baths on a given day.

The facility also had a theater, three restaurants, and a museum that displayed objects of curiosity, such as Egyptian mummies, a tiny trunk full of miniature clothing worn by the famous dwarf Tom Thumb, and a model carnival created from toothpicks by a San Quentin inmate.

With his knack for bringing health and pleasure to the population, it's not hard to understand why, for awhile, Adolph Sutro was the most popular man in San Francisco.

81. The Lions of Sutro Heights

This lion—one of two—at the entry to Sutro Heights at 46th Avenue and the Great Highway, is one of the few remaining artifacts of the estate of Adolph Sutro, developer, mayor of San Francisco, and philanthropist.

Although his name is associated with the mining of the Comstock Lode in Nevada, Sutro did not acquire his fortune as a miner. Rather, he devised a plan for the mines that would make him rich and also save lives. Recognizing that silver mining at the mountainous Nevada site was difficult and dangerous because the shafts regularly filled with water, Sutro forged an idea for a passage through the terrain that would drain millions of gallons. His project had been no easy task. Between the time he launched his project in 1865 and its completion in 1879, he developed a reputation for one-note advocacy that awarded him the moniker "The Great Bore."

In the 1880s, Sutro was able to sell his creation at a very significant profit, taking advantage of his buyers' lack of understanding that the Comstock Lode silver rush was pretty much a thing of the past. He returned to San Francisco with enough of a bankroll to buy one-twelfth of the land in San Francisco, including the landmarks we now know as Mount Sutro, Sutro Forest, and Sutro Heights.

On the heights, Sutro built a spacious, turreted mansion that he stocked with 125,000 rare and valuable books. He landscaped the premises with expansive lawns. Fawns grazed, and the grounds were sprinkled with hundreds of plaster copies of the great sculptures of antiquity, a few of which are still on display. The art critics scoffed at these reproductions, but the public that Sutro admitted to the gardens for 10-cents each delighted in the total experience of flowers, art, and vistas. He augmented this visitor experience by battling the Southern Pacific Railroad that had monopolized the city's transportation system. Developing his own line, he was able to provide railway transportation to the Gardens and the nearby Sutro Baths for the reduced fare of a nickel.

Because of this magnanimity, Sutro gained a deserved reputation as a man of the people when the city was facing one of its periodic epidemics of civic corruption. He was prevailed upon to run for mayor in 1894. Alas, he served only one term. The man who owned a big hunk of the city's land, was, despite his progressive instincts, really not cut out to spearhead a reform agenda.

Sutro died in 1898. Upon cremation, his ashes were transported to a crypt at the San Francisco Columbarium. Some years later, they turned up missing. Then

in 1979, when Sutro's oceanfront property had become part of the Golden Gate National Recreation Area, a National Park Service ranger found a 14-inch high marble urn on a ledge 25 feet below the heights. Could these be the ashes of Adolph Sutro? We probably will never know because the urn was turned over to Sutro's heirs unexamined. If the urn did contain his remains, the discovery would have corresponded with Sutro's dying wish: "Bury me where I can watch the ocean and Seal Rocks. Bury me at Sutro Heights."

82. The Audiffred Building

L ocated on the west side of the Embarcadero, this 19th-century structure, echoing perfectly the ambience of old-time Paris, seems very much a beautiful odd duck. Except for the 1898 Ferry Building, the Audiffred Building, erected in 1889 at the terminus of Mission Street, is the only waterfront survivor of the 1906 earthquake and fire.

The building's survival was not just the luck of the draw. Rather it's here because of a quick-thinking barkeep appealing to the needs of booze-parched first-responders. In April 1906, San Francisco firemen were busy dynamiting buildings along the west side of the Embarcadero. The plan was to bring down the structures in order to stop the progress of the fire and save the accumulating supplies on the east side of the thoroughfare. As the dynamiters began placing explosives at the Audiffred Building, the alarmed barman at the Bulkhead Saloon, which occupied the ground floor of the building, advanced a proposition: Let the building stand and we will reward you with a horse cart full of wine and two quarts of whiskey each. The firemen bought in, and, thus fortified, fought the flames for three days, saving the building.

The Audiffred was the property of one Hippolite d'Audiffred, a Frenchman. Audiffred had arrived in San Francisco by a circuitous route. In 1850, at age 20, he left France to seek his fortune in Mexico. Alas, it was not a good time to be French in that country. The French-installed Emperor Maximilian had alienated enough of the locals that they struck back and executed him. Discretion being the better part of valor, Audiffred realized it was time to move on. He bought a donkey, loaded it with his belongings, and made the 2,500-mile trek to San Francisco.

With a shrewd mind for moneymaking, Audiffred established a niche enterprise, selling charcoal to Chinese laundries. Now, prosperous but homesick, he set out to erect a building that reminded him of his beloved Paris. His building had a mansard roof with a garret, and tall, round-topped windows decorated with heavy brick crenellation. Ever since, it's been a Francophile's delight.

However, in addition to its longevity and uniqueness, the Audiffred Building has other components that have contributed to its landmark designation. The buildings first tenant—in addition to three saloons and a restaurant—was the Coast Seaman's Union, which battled intransigent shipowners to become the first permanent sailor's union in history. Today the sidewalk in front of the building serves as an inconspicuous memorial to the events of Bloody Thursday, July 5, 1934, when two unionists supporting the maritime strike called by the Longshoremen's Association were gunned down by police.

By the 1950s, the neighborhood around the Audiffred Building had turned seedy, a condition not helped when the four-story Embarcadero Freeway went up next door. In 1979, when the building was pretty much done in by damage from a broken gas main, the structure was scheduled for demolition. Alerted preservationists sounded the alarm. The building was declared a San Francisco landmark, placed on the National Register of Historic Places and restored, a process aided by the demolition of the freeway in 1989.

The street level of the Audiffred Building had long been home to a series of saloons where the uninitiated had better not look the wrong way. Since 1993, however, this space has housed the elegant Boulevard restaurant. Few examples of gentrification have been so conspicuous.

Why Is This There?

83. Sutro Tower

I n 1970, San Franciscans had a choice. They could keep abreast of the TV exploits of *Dr. Marcus Welby, M.D.*, or they could nix a 997-foot antenna atop an 817-foot mountain, the entire structure towering 1,814 above sea level. The doctor won out. Sutro Tower went ahead.

Before the tower, San Francisco's hill-filled topography allowed for very spotty television reception. The tower was meant to correct that and provide all citizens with equal access to Ultra Ban 5000 commercials.

Actually, it's not quite correct to say that San Franciscans had a choice. The project, approved in 1967, began construction in 1971 and was completed in 1973, and was well underway before anyone was paying much attention. That's because the tower was the baby of the major local TV stations, including KRON owned by the Chronicle Broadcasting Co. One need not be a conspiracy theorist to understand that the stations were eager to get the project going in order to fend off the cable revolution coming over the not-too-distant horizon. Thus, the media moguls, reasonably enough, did not place tower developments as the lead story on the 10 o'clock news.

As the tower began to rise there was something of an uproar. Planning Director Allan Jacobs said that the tower was "pretty terrible—aesthetically, environmentally and from about every standpoint you can imagine," but he had not been planning director in 1967 when the project was approved.

Dianne Feinstein, then a San Francisco supervisor, said the tower was "undoubtedly one of the worst structures, visually, I have had an opportunity to view."

Herb Caen feared that the creature, reminiscent of nothing so much as a robotic villain from a '50s sci-fi flick, would "stalk down the hill and attack the Golden Gate Bridge."

But the construction ball was rolling and unstoppable. Now, more than 35 years later, the tower, San Francisco's most visible landmark when approaching the city from the east or south, is accepted by most and even loved by a few.

What's This?

84. Bloody Thursday
Commemoration Mural/Sculpture

This piece at the corner of Mission and Steuart Streets, executed by a group of artists who called themselves Mural Environmentalists Together in Art Labor, is not easy to decipher without a program. The flowing piece, made up of three irregularly shaped steel panels evoking the sea, is placed near the spot where Howard Sperry, a longshoreman, and Nick Bordoise, a cook, were gunned down on Bloody Thursday, July 5, 1934, a seminal event in the waterfront strike of that year. Some 31 other strikers were badly bloodied on that day. Sperry and Bordoise are here depicted with red faces. The police aren't hard to spot. They're the ones in pie-plate helmets on rearing horses, wearing gas masks.

A few days following that Sunday, 40,000 people participated in a silent memorial parade up Market Street. A General Strike of thousands of Bay Area workers was called. For three days, restaurants, gas stations, and grocery stores closed. But the strike's momentum began to wither when mainstream labor leaders refused to support it. According to historian Chris Carlsson, the San Francisco Labor Council went so far as to issue a work permit to striking sheet-metal workers to return to their jobs in order to repair bullet-riddled police cars.

By the end of the month, the strike had been submitted to arbitration and the workers won a major demand, an end to the "shape up" (depicted on the back of the sculpture-mural) where workers had to endure the humiliating exercise of each morning submitting to the bosses' cherry-picking of workers, who often had to bribe their way into a job that paid 75 cents an hour for an 8-a.m.-to-midnight shift. The shape up was replaced with a hiring hall that gave the union considerable control over hiring and work rules

Most importantly, the waterfront strike of 1934 demonstrated to employers and workers alike the power of collective action. For many years thereafter, San Francisco was known as a union town.

What's This?

85. Hearst Building

This letter "H" on the Julia Morgan-designed entrance to the Hearst Building, at the southeast corner of Third and Market Streets is about the only reminder we have of the down-and-dirty newspaper wars that dominated this intersection around the turn of the last century. This is the birthplace of the *San Francisco Examiner,* the first publication in the Hearst newspaper empire. On the southwest corner was the headquarters of the *San Francisco Call* and on the eastern corner of Kearny and Market, the *Chronicle* building—now restored as a Ritz Carlton residence club.

It was the 24-year-old William Randolph Hearst who in 1887 stirred the pot that started the competition. That was the year the recently expelled Harvard student, became "proprietor," as he called it, of the moribund *Examiner.* The newspaper came as a gift from his father, George Hearst, a man who had struck it rich in the Comstock Lode. It is said, he won the paper in a poker game.

"Willy" as he was known, plunged into his new responsibility with great enthusiasm, working 15 hours a day. He saw the local papers as totally out of touch with the city's changing demographics, relying as they did on front page stories of saloon fights and ads for patent medicines. He said he wanted to create a paper that would leave the gripman coming to work on the Powell Street cable car line at 4 o'clock in the morning muttering, "Gee whiz."

He fired a shot across the bow of the competition by christening the *Examiner* the "Monarch of the Dailies." Next he gave the paper a whole new look, enlarging headlines and the size of the type, reducing the intimidating number of nine columns to seven, and greatly increasing the number of illustrations to help less than proficient readers through the text.

When he couldn't find news, he would invent it. Typically, hearing about deplorable conditions at the City Receiving Hospital, he called on one of his "sob sister" reporters, so named for their ability to create stories that reduced readers to tears. The job went this time to one Annie, who, disguised as an indigent,

collapsed on Kearny Street and was admitted to the Receiving Hospital. She was able to report on the hospital's gross cruelty and neglect, resulting in the wholesale dismissal of the staff.

As part of his reformist mission, Hearst saw his job as giving the police a helping hand. "Whenever a child is to be found, an eloping girl to be brought home, or a murder to be traced, one of our staff is sure to give the sleepy detectives their first pointers," he editorialized.

The *Examiner* had none of the reactionary patina that came to characterize Hearst publications in later decades. The paper's editorials supported organized labor, took on the greedy railroads, and proselytized for the 8-hour-day.

By 1895, Hearst was looking for bigger fish to fry. He moved to New York, took over the *New York Journal,* and embarked on the journey that created the Hearst media conglomerate we know today.

The *Examiner,* however, was never far from Hearst's attention. Until his death in 1951, he maintained a residence on the top floor of the Third and Market building. The newspaper remained at the site until 1965. The free San Francisco newspaper now publishing as the *Examiner* has nothing to do with William Randolph Hearst.

What Happed to…?

86. Playland at the Beach

This plaque, set amidst a bit of green space in a 1970s condo development where Playland at the Beach once stood, is the only reminder of the oceanfront good times of a previous era.

The amusement park thrived for 50 years, but by the 1960s the site had grown seedy. Muggings, vandalism, and petty crime were driving patrons away. The wrecking ball fell in 1972.

There had been amusements at the beach since the 1890s when trolleys began transporting San Franciscans from the city's cheek-to-jowl center to the fresh breezes and oceanfront open space. Individual concessioners set up shooting galleries and baseball throws. There was a Ferris wheel and an early rollercoaster called "Gravity's Rainbow."

In 1926, George Whitney was brought in to manage the diverse businesses. During the Depression years of the 1930s, as the concessions began floundering, Whitney saw a chance to acquire them one by one, thus consolidating his holdings to create Playland at the Beach.

During World War II, as residents stayed close to home and thousands of servicemen passed through the city, the amusement park thrived, a momentum that continued into the 1950s.

When Playland finally did call it quits, it left behind memories of getting lost in the Fun House mirror maze, maneuvering through the Topsy Turvy Barrel, which left the uninitiated on their backs, and climbing three stories to descend on what was advertised as "the longest and bumpiest indoor slide in the world."

Playland's merry-go-round, now a prominent feature of the Yerba Buena Center, featured handcarved prancing horses four abreast, necks arched and manes flowing. Kids mounted on these steeds would reach for the brass ring, which they would either attempt to throw back into the open mouth of a grinning clown head, or pocket to add to their collection. In one year, the concessionaire reported losing 70,000 rings.

Playland was not without its real and imaginary dangers. Everyone knew the story of the sailor who was decapitated by the crossbar as he stood up on the Big Dipper roller coaster, his sliced-off head falling into the lap of a lady in the car below. Everyone had heard the story from a friend of a friend of someone who was eyewitness to the gruesome event.

Former Playland denizens also remember the food. Not only the usual amusement park fare, but the It's-It, invented by George Whitney. Playland was the only place in America where one could purchase this decadent concoction of vanilla ice cream sandwiched between two large oatmeal cookies and dipped in chocolate. When Playland was demolished, It's-It lived on and is now distributed in several states.

Remnants of Playland remain scattered throughout the Bay Area, at places such as Fisherman's Wharf and the Santa Cruz Boardwalk. Perhaps none of these artifacts is more jolting to those who had been there than the incarnations of the gap-toothed, red-headed, papier-mâché figure, Laughing Sal, whose hideous cackle was launched from the front window of the Fun House. Many adults, who as small children were afraid of Sal, remember her now as the Good Witch overseeing a fairy land that will never return.

HISTORICAL SITE

ON THIS SITE, FROM SUTRO HEIGHTS PARK
TO GOLDEN GATE PARK, FROM THE
EARLY 1920s UNTIL 1972, STOOD THE
WORLD-FAMOUS PLAYLAND-AT-THE-BEACH
AMUSEMENT PARK. THIS MONUMENT IS
FONDLY DEDICATED TO THE REMEMBRANCE
OF THOSE DAYS OF FUN AND LAUGHTER
AT THE BEACH.

DEDICATED MAY 19, 1981
BY
DIANNE G. FEINSTEIN, MAYOR
CITY & COUNTY OF SAN FRANCISCO

PRESENTED BY
TAL, PRESIDENT
IGH ASSOCIATES

About the Author

Art Peterson, a lifelong Bay Area resident, taught in the San Francisco public schools for 30 years, 15 of these as a teacher of writing at Lowell High School. Until recently, he was employed as Senior Editor at the University of California-affiliated National Writing Project, the nation's prime organization devoted to the teaching of writing in the schools.

He is the author of several books, including the best-selling humor book *Teachers: A Survival Guide for the Grownup in the Classroom,* and the teaching classic, *The Writer's Workout Book: 113 Stretches Toward Better Prose.*

For seven years he edited the Telegraph Hill Dwellers' *Semaphore.* He is a member of the San Francisco Museum and Historical Society and the California Historical Society

With his wife Carol, he lives in San Francisco, just a stone's throw from the Transamerica Pyramid (2) the Colombo Market Arch (30), and the Old Ship Saloon (18).

Photo Credits

All photos not on this list are by Art Peterson.

p. 21: Alcatraz (top), Chris Carlsson

p. 28-29: Seals Stadium, San Francisco History Center, San Francisco Public Library (AAC-5448)

p. 46: Japanese Tea Garden, web

p. 47: Palace of Fine Arts, from original souvenir publication

p. 51: Roscoe "Fatty" Arbuckle, web

p. 51: Roscoe "Fatty" Arbuckle, mug shot, San Francisco Police Department

p. 54: Detail of Sirron Norris mural, Chris Carlsson

p. 54: Balmy Alley mural, Patricia Rodriguez

p. 64: 1912 Ferries at Ferry Building, Foundsf.org

p. 67: Abe Ruef (upper right) Wikimedia Commons

p. 67: Abe Ruef getting advice from attorney Henry Achs, Bancroft Library/Sunsite: I0041476A

p. 69: Bay to Breakers photos, Huffington Post contest online

p. 77: HUAC hosing on City Hall steps, San Francisco History Center, San Francisco Public Library (AAF-1023)

p. 80: Inner Telegraph Station, The Annals of San Francisco, 1855

p. 87: Colombo Market, California Historical Society/Foundsf.org

p. 94: Patty Hearst in Hibernia Bank, Wikimedia Commons

p. 99: *City Life* mural images, Lacadez, via Flickr.com

p. 107: East side of Telegraph Hill, Chris Carlsson

p. 114: Long view of Angel Island, Chris Carlsson

p. 117: Inset photo of Harvey Milk, Crawford Barton/Foundsf.org

p. 121: Spite Fence, Edweard Muybridge/Foundsf.org

p. 124: Fontana Towers, Chris Carlsson

p. 127: Harry Bridges at 1939 Labor Day March, ILWU archives

p. 131: Courtesy of Macchirini Creative Design. Photo by Peter Macchirini

p. 132: Emperor Norton on a bike, Foundsf.org

p. 136: A. P. Giannini, web

p. 139: 1958 aerial of Embarcadero Freeway, Foundsf.org

p. 141: George Christopher and Benny Bufano, *The Semaphore*

p. 151: Fog rolling in, Chris Carlsson

p. 155: Dykes on Bikes, Chris Carlsson

p. 156: Chinese New Year, Gainer Donnelly

p. 157: Chinese New Year, Anomalous_A, via Flickr.com

p. 159: Carnaval (top), Chris Carlsson

p. 159: Cinco de Mayo, Irene, via Flickr.com

p. 161: Sheriff Richard Hongisto at I-Hotel, Calvin Roberts/Granma's Camera

p. 175: Hippodrome (top), San Francisco History Center, San Francisco Public Library (AAB-1205)

p. 175: Hippodrome (bottom), San Francisco History Center, San Francisco Public Library (AAB-1204)

p. 178: Condor club (right), San Francisco History Center, S.F. Public Library (AAB-2968)

p. 178: Carol Doda ad, web

p. 180: Robert Arneson sculpture, San Francisco Museum of Modern Art/ Robert Arneson Foundation

p. 187: Woodward's Gardens, by T. E. Hecht 1875/Foundsf.org

p. 189: Mary Ellen Pleasant's trees, Chris Carlsson

p. 190: Mary Ellen Pleasant, Foundsf.org

p.195: Treasure Island under construction 1938, Foundsf.org

p. 197: Parrots, Chris Carlsson

p. 198: Fog photos, Chris Carlsson

p. 211: Sutro Baths (large photo), Chris Carlsson

p. 213: Adolph Sutro portrait, San Francisco History Center, San Francisco Public Library (AAD-3219)

p. 217: Sutro Tower, Chris Carlsson

p. 219: Bordoise and Sperry down, ILWU archives

p. 221: Hearst Building, Chris Carlsson

p. 224: Playland roller coaster, Kurt Bank

Bibliography

Books

Accardi, Catherine. *San Francisco Landmarks.* Charleston, South Carolina: Arcadia Publishing, 2012.

———. *San Francisco's North Beach and Telegraph Hill.* Charleston, South Carolina: Arcadia Publishing, 2010.

Adams, Charles F. *The Magnificent Rogues of San Francisco.* Palo Alto, California: Pacific Books, 1998.

Asbury, Herbert. *The Barbary Coast: An Informal History of the San Francisco Underworld.* New York: Alfred A. Knopf, 1933.

Bacon, Daniel. *Walking San Francisco on the Barbary Coast Trail.* San Francisco, California: Quicksilver Press, 1995.

Bakalinsky, Adah. *Stairway Walks in San Francisco: The Joy of Urban Exploring.* (7th Edition). Birmingham, Alabama: Wilderness Press, 2010.

Boulware, Jack. *San Francisco Bizarro: A Guide to Notorious Sites, Lusty Pursuits, and Downright Freakiness in the City by the Bay.* New York: St. Martin's Press, 2000.

Boyd, Dick. *Broadway North Beach: The Golden Years, A Saloon Keepers Tales.* San Francisco, California: Cape Foundation Publications, 2006.

Brook, James, Chris Carlsson, and Nancy J. Peters (eds.). *Reclaiming San Francisco History Politics Culture.* San Francisco, California: City Lights Books, 1998.

Caen, Herb. *The Best of Herb Caen.* San Francisco, California: Chronicle Books, 1991.

———. *Herb Caen's San Francisco: 1976-1991.* San Francisco, California: Chronicle Books, 1992.

Cass, Maxine. *It Happened in San Francisco.* Guilford, Connecticut: Morris Book Publishing, 2006.

Cole, Tom. *A Short History of San Francisco.* San Francisco, California: Lexicos, 1981.

Corbett, Michael. *Splendid Survivors: San Francisco's Downtown Architectural Heritage.* San Francisco: California Living Books, 1979.

Delehanty, Randolph. *The Ultimate Guide: San Francisco.* San Francisco, California: Chronicle Books, 1989.

Dillon, Richard. *North Beach: The Italian Heart of San Francisco.* Novato, California: Presidio Press, 1985.

Doss, Margot Patterson. *Golden Gate Park at Your Feet.* San Rafael, California: Presidio Press, 1978.

Downs, Tom. *Walking San Francisco.* Birmingham, Alabama: ReadHowYouWant Press 2012.

Dunlap, Carol. *California People.* Salt Lake City: Peregrine Smith Books, 1982.

Edmonds, Andy. *Frame-Up! :The Shocking Scandal that Destroyed Hollywood's Biggest Comedy Star Roscoe "Fatty" Arbuckle.* New York: Avon Books, 1992.

Fradkin, Phillip, L. *The Great Earthquake and Firestorms of 1906*. Berkeley, California: University of California Press, 2005.

Friedman, Steven (ed.). *Golden Memories of the San Francisco Bay Area*. Charleston, South Carolina, Arcadia Publishing, 2000.

Gentry, Curt. *The Madams of San Francisco An Irreverent History of the City by the Golden Gate*. New York: Ballantine Books, 1964.

Gilliam, Harold. *Weather of the San Francisco Bay Region*. Berkeley, California: University of California Press, 2002.

Goupil, Helene and Josh Krist. *San Francisco: The Unknown City*. Vancouver B.C.: Arsenal Pulp Press, 2005.

Herron, Don. *The Dashiell Hammett Tour. Thirtieth Anniversary Guidebook*. San Francisco, California: Vince Emory Productions, 2009.

————. *The Literary World of San Francisco & Its Environs*. San Francisco: City Lights Books, 1985.

Hudson, Lynn M. *The Making of "Mammy" Pleasant: A Black Entrepreneur in Nineteenth-Century San Francisco*. Urbana, Illinois: University of Illinois Press, 2003.

Kamiya, Gary. *Cool Gray City of Love: 49 Views of San Francisco*. New York: Bloomsbury, 2013.

King John. *Cityscapes: San Francisco and its Buildings*. Berkeley, California: Heyday Press, 2011.

Lewis, Oscar and Carroll D. Hall. *Bonanza Inn: America's First Luxury Hotel*. New York: Ballantine Books, 1971.

————. *San Francisco: Mission to Metropolis*. Berkeley, California: Howell-North Books, 1966.

————. *The Big Four: The Story of Huntington, Stanford, Hopkins, and Crocker, and of the Building of the Central Pacific*. New York: ALfred A. Knopf, 1938.

Myrick, David F. *San Francisco's Telegraph Hill*. San Francisco: City Lights Foundation, 2001.

Montanarelli, Lisa and Ann Harrison. *Strange But True: San Francisco*. London: PRC Publishing, 2005.

Moore, Sarah J. *Empire on Display: San Francisco's Panama-Pacific International Exposition of 1915*. Norman, Oklahoma: University of Oklahoma Press, 2013.

Mullen, Kevin J. *Chinatown Squad: Policing the Dragon From the Gold Rush to the 21st Century*. Novato, California: Noir Publications, 2008.

Olmsted, Nancy. *The Ferry Building: Witness to a Century of Change, 1898-1998*. San Francisco: Heyday Books, 1998.

Olmsted, Roger and T. H. Watkins. *Here Today: San Francisco's Architectural Heritage*. San Francisco: Chronicle Books, 1968.

Ralston, John C. *This Date in San Francisco: 366 Days in the History of Our Fascinating Beloved City*. Mountain View, California: RIW Publishing, 2011.

Richards, Rand. *Historic San Francisco: A Concise History and Guide*. San Francisco: Heritage House Publishers, 1991.

———. *Historic Walks in San Francisco: 18 Trails Through the City's Past*. San Francisco: Heritage House Publishers, 2002.

Starr, Kevin. *Golden Gate The Life and Times of America's Greatest Bridge*. New York: Bloomsbury Publishing, 2010.

———. *The Dream Endures: California Enters the 1940s*. New York: Oxford University Press, 1997.

———. *Embattled Dreams: California in War and Peace, 1940-1950*. New York: Oxford University Press, 2002.

Smith, James R. *San Francisco's Lost Landmarks*. Sanger, California: Word Dancer Press, 2005.

Swan, Christopher. *Cable Car*. Berkeley, California: Ten Speed Press, 1973.

Talbot, David. *Season of the Witch: Enchantment, Terror, and Deliverance in the City of Love*. New York: Free Press, 2012.

Thomas, Lately. *A Debonair Scoundrel: An Episode in the Moral History of San Francisco, The Flamboyant Story of Abe Ruef*. New York: Holt Rinehart and Winston, 1962.

Trimble, Paul C. and William Knorp *Ferries of San Francisco Bay*. Charleston, South Carolina: Arcadia Publishing, 2007.

Wels, Susan. *San Francisco: Arts for the City—Civic Art and Urban Change, 1932-2012*. Berkeley, California: Heyday, 2013.

Wiley, Peter Booth. *National Trust Guide: San Francisco, America's Guide for Architecture and History Travelers*. New York: John Wiley and Sons, Inc., 2000.

Zakheim, Masha. *Coit Tower San Francisco: Its History and Art*. Volcano, California: Volcano Press, 2009

Newspapers

San Francisco Chronicle, 1979-1989.

San Francisco Examiner, 1979-1989.

Online Resources

foundsf.org

sfhistoryencyclopedia.com

sfcityguides.org

shapingsf.org

sparkletack.com

232

Index

Events

1894 Midwinter International
Exposition 45, 193

1915 Panama Pacific International Exposition
.... 37, 47, 148, 193, 228

1939 Golden Gate International Exposition .. 193

1961 All-Star Game 151

1964 Republican National Convention 176

1989 Loma Prieta earthquake 31, 49, 137, 149

Bay to Breakers 68

Bloody Thursday, July 5, 1934 218

Carnaval 158

Chinese Exclusion Act of 1882 113

Chinese New Year 156

Cinco de Mayo 158

Civil War 145

Comstock Lode silver rush 210, 212

Earthquake and fire of 1906 ...... 49, 58, 68, 81, 89,
134, 165, 209

Free Speech Movement 77

Gay Freedom Day Parade 154

Gold Rush.. 17, 49, 55, 131, 145, 171, 203, 228

San Francisco Lesbian, Gay, Bisexual, and Transgender Pride Celebration 154

Spanish-American War 35

Media

Alta California newspaper 79

Associated Press 111

Black Mask magazine 73

KRON-TV 216

Los Angeles Times 176

New York Journal 222

Overland Monthly 25, 45

People's Daily 191

Ramparts magazine 130

San Francisco Bulletin 133

San Francisco Call 220

San Francisco Chronicle 35, 45, 137, 199, 229

San Francisco Examiner 43, 92, 124, 173,
220, 222, 229

The New Masses 100

Western Brewer magazine 184

Movies

Invasion of the Body Snatchers 12

Operation Abolition 77

Pal Joey 175

Star Wars 168

The Love Bug 166

The Maltese Falcon 73

The Wild Parrots of Telegraph Hill 196

Vertigo 109

What's Up, Doc? 166

Zodiac 12

Organizations

American Civil Liberties Union 200

American Jewish Congress 200

Americans United for Separation of Church
and State 200

Anchor Steam Beer 184

Bank of America 134, 136, 153

Bank of California 208

Bank of Italy 134, 136

Board of Public Works 106

Bureau of Prisons 19

Church of Scientology 11

Coast Seaman's Union 214

Communist Party 75

Council of Armenian-American Organizations
of Northern California 200

Crocker Bank 101

Dykes on Bikes 154

Four Seas Corporation 162

House Un-American Activities Committee
(HUAC) 75

International Longshore and Warehouse Union
(ILWU) 126

International Longshoremen's Association 98

Keystone Studios 50

Kink.com 170

Kuomintang 191

Lloyd's of London 176

Mujeres Muralistas 53, 54

Mural Environmentalists Together
  in Art Labor 218

National Guard 19, 168

National Park Service 114, 213

National Register of Historic
  Places 42, 168, 215

Neptune Society 109

OddFellows Fraternal Organization 109

Parents, Families and Friends of Lesbians
  and Gays (PFLAG) 154

Precita Eyes 54

Public Works Art Project (PWAP) 98

San Francisco 49ers 129

San Francisco Giants 27, 150

San Francisco Heritage 43

San Francisco Merchants Association 106

San Francisco Planning Commission 11

San Francisco Real Estate Board 25

San Francisco Seals 27

Sierra Club 9

South End Rowing Club 20

Southern Pacific Railroad 62, 65, 212

Spring Valley Water Co. 38

Symbionese Liberation Army (SLA) 92

The Willing Circle 106

Union Labor Party 65

United Farm Workers 53, 158

United Nations 111, 158

University of California 65, 77, 92, 172,
                                                    226, 228

U.S. Marines 19

U.S. Navy 104, 116

W. & J. Sloane 208

People

Agnos, Art 128, 137

Aitken, Robert 35

Albert, Frankie 129

Alioto, Joseph 11, 128, 140

Anthony, Joe 55

Appelgarth, George 149

Arbuckle, Roscoe "Fatty" 50

Arnautoff, Victor 98

Arneson, Robert 179, 181

Ashe, Elizabeth 106

Atherton, Gertrude 97

Badlam, Alexander 204

Bailey, F. Lee 94

Barnes, Fannie Mae 14

Bell, Thomas 190

Benezra, Neal 181

Benny, Jack 193

Bernhardt, Sarah 22

Bilbrey, Braxton 20

Bittner, Mark 196

Bordoise, Nick 218

Boudin, Isadore 17

Brady, Matthew 50

Brekle, Gottlieb 184

Bridges, Harry 126, 128, 140

Brodie, John 129

Brown, Arthur, Jr. 41, 62, 97

Brown, John 190

Brown, Madie 200

Brown, Willie 83

Buchanan, James 182

Buchanan, John 182

Bufano, Beniamino 140, 141, 191

Buffalo Bill 22

Burton, Phillip 9, 10, 109

Bush, J. B. 182

Caen, Herb 64, 134, 199, 216, 227

Cameron, Donaldina 70, 72

Carlsson, Chris 218

Carter, Jimmy 94

Cepeda, Orlando 27

Chavez, Cesar 53, 158

Christopher, George 27, 141, 154, 229

Church, Frank 162

Churchill, Winston 111

Clinton, Bill 94

Coit, Howard 95

Coit, Lillie Hitchcock 95, 98

Cosby, Bill 166

Crabtree, Lotta 163

Crocker, Charles 119

Crowley, Patrick 133

d'Audiffred, Hippolite 214

Davis, Jacob 171

DeFreeze, Donald 92

Delmont, Maude 50

Demoro, Harry 62

Dewey, George 35

de Young, Michael 35, 45, 46

DiMaggio, Joe 27

Doda, Carol 176, 178

Duer, John K. 79

Dumas, Alexander 163

Eddy, William 182

Edison, Thomas 103

Eli, Look Tin 25, 26

Empress Dowager 25

Farnsworth, Philo T. 101, 103

Feinstein, Dianne 139, 162, 179, 181, 216

Ferlinghetti, Lawrence 73

Fitch, George 133

Fleishhacker, Herbert 95

Flood, James 119

Ford, Henry 49

Foster, Marcus 92

Fremont, John C. 104

Fry, Roger 140

Gernreich, Rudi 176

Giannini, A. P. 134, 136, 153

Gilliam, Harold 150, 228

Goldwater, Barry 116

Goodman, Benny 193

Gough, Charles 182

Gray, George 106, 108

Gray, Harry 106

Griffith, Alice 106

Guevara, Che 92

Hagiwara, Makoto 46

Hallidie, Andrew 14

Hall, William Hammond 14, 38, 77, 81, 83, 116, 118, 140

Hammett, Dashiell 73, 74, 207

Happersberger, Frank 81, 83

Harding, Florence 122

Harding, Warren G. 122

Harrison, Benjamin 22

Hayworth, Rita 175

Hearst, George 220

Hearst, Patricia 92

Hearst, Phoebe Apperson 47

Hearst, Randolph 92

Hearst, William Randolph 173, 220, 222

Heil, Walter, Dr. 98, 100

Hitler, Adolf 111, 195

Hodges, Russ 27

Hongisto, Richard 161, 162

Hopkins, Mark 119

Huntington, Collis 119

Iverson, George 101

Jacobs, Allan 216

Jacobs, John 9

Johnson, Phillip 41

Johnson, Walter 47

Jones, Jim, Rev. 179

Keating, Edward 130

Kelham, George 200

Kelly, Shanghai 57

Kennedy, Robert 140

Kezar, Mary E. 129

King Ludwig of Bavaria 163

King, Martin Luther, Jr. 140

Klussman, Friedel 14

Langdon, William 67

Lapham, Roger 14

Leno, Mark 84

Lick, James 81

Liszt, Franz 163

Lloyd, Benjamin Estelle 173

Lococo, Joe 108

Macchiarini, Peter 131

Marichal, Juan 27

Mason, Marsden 9, 14, 89, 91

Mattei, Peter 124

Maybeck, Bernard 47, 49

Mays, Willie 27

Maytag, Fritz 184

McCoppin, Frank 38

McCovey, Willie 27

McElhenny, Hugh 129

McLaren, John 22, 33, 34, 38, 46

Milk, Harvey 116, 117, 118, 179

Miller, Stu 151

Molinari, John 166

Montez, Lola 163

Moore, Dorothea, Dr. 106

Moose, Ed 203

Morabito, Tony 129

Morgan, Julia 220

Morrow, Irving 104

Moscone, George 116, 162, 179, 181

Murphy, Samuel 38

Mussolini, Benito 195

Nagare, Masayuki 134

Napoleon III 95

Newhall, Scott 137

Nixon, Richard 9, 50, 147

Norris, Frank 184

Norris, Sirron 54

Norton, Joshua "Emperor" 131

Novak, Kim 175

O'Farrell, Jasper 182

Olmsted, Frederick Law 38, 228

O'Malley, Walter 27

Osborne, Fanny 142

Page, Charles Hall 43

Parks, Rosa 190

Pegler, Westbrook 140

Pereira, William 11

Perry, Joe 129

Piper, George 142

Pleasant, Mary Ellen "Mammy". 4, 188, 190, 228

Polk, Willis 142

Porter, Bruce 142

Ralston, William 208, 228

Rand, Sally 193, 228

Rappe, Virginia 50

Reagan, Ronald 92, 124

Richardson, Bobby 29

Rivera, Diego 98

Rockefeller, Nelson 128

Rodin, Auguste 148

Rodriguez, Patricia 53

Rolph, "Sunny Jim" 122

Roosevelt, Franklin D. 98, 111, 200

Roosevelt, Theodore 65

Rosenberg, "Big Davey" 176, 178

Rossi, Angelo 200

Ruef, Abe 65, 67, 106

Sarnoff, David 101, 103

Schmitz, Eugene 58, 65, 67

Schulz, Charles 29

Shelley, John 178

Shorenstein, Walter 162

Sinatra, Frank 175

Sperry, Howard 218

Spreckels, Adolph 35, 148

Spreckels, Alma 35, 148

Spreckels, Claus 35

Stalin, Joseph 111, 128

Stanford, Leland 119

Steel, Danielle 37

Stettinius, Edward 111

Stevenson, Robert Louis 142

Stoneham, Horace 27

Strauss, Joseph 147, 152, 153

Strauss, Levi 171

Sun Yat-sen 191

Sutro, Adolph 210, 212

Tadich, John 204

Temko, Alan 31, 60

Terry, Ralph 27

Thomas, Jerry 203

Tittle, Y. A. 129

Truman, Harry 111, 112

Vaillancourt, Armand 31, 32

Verdier, Felix 41

Warneke, John Carl 41
Watson, Willie 122
Wayburn, Edgar 9
Weinberger, Caspar 124
Wheeler, William 75
White, Dan 116, 179
Whitney, George 223
Wight, Clifford 100
Wiley, Peter Booth 11, 229
Willis, Edwin 75
Wilson, Billy 129
Wilson, Woodrow 140
Woodward, Robert 186
Wright, Frank Lloyd 60
Yung, Nicholas 119
Ziegfield, Florenz 50

Places

Alamo Square 68
Alcatraz 19, 20, 55
Alemany Gap 150
Angel Island 19, 113, 114
Aquatic Park 20, 62, 124
Armory 168, 170
Asian Art Museum 81
Audiffred Building 214, 215
Balmy Alley 53, 54
Barbary Coast 35, 55, 173, 227
Bataan Lunch 160
Bayview District 86
Blanco's Bar 160
Cameron House 70, 71, 72
Candlestick Park 27, 130, 150
Chinatown . 25, 26, 70, 137, 142, 191, 192, 228
City Lights Book Shop 73
City of Paris 41, 42, 43
Cliff House 199
Coit Tower 5, 95, 98, 100, 196, 229
Colombo Market Arch 86, 87, 226
Columbarium 109, 110, 212
Columbus Tower 65
Comstock Saloon 131

Condor Club 176
Corona Heights 106
Cow Palace 94
Double Play bar 27
Duboce Park 118
Embarcadero Freeway 31, 64, 137, 215
Fairmont Hotel 11, 111
Ferry Building .. 62, 64, 126, 137, 196, 214, 228
Fillmore District 86
Fort Mason 9
Fort Point 49, 145, 146, 147
Fourth Street Bridge 152
Golden Gate Bridge 5, 9, 11, 62, 104,
136, 137, 147, 152, 193, 216
Golden Gate National Recreation Area 9, 109,
213
Golden Gate Park 5, 22, 23,
25, 33, 38, 45, 68, 129, 208, 227
Japanese Tea Garden 45, 46
Grace Cathedral 119, 120, 121
Grass Valley 163
Guyana 179
Hearst Building 220
Hippodrome 173, 175
Hobart Building 101
hungry i 166
Hunters Point 25
Hyde Street Pier 62
International Hotel (I-Hotel) 160, 162
Kezar Stadium 129
Lake Merced 86
Le Petit Trianon 148, 149
Levi's Plaza 171
Lombard Street 5, 166
Lotta's Fountain 163, 165
Maiden Lane 60
Main Library 81
Mango's Smoke Shop 160
Manilatown 160, 162
Marina District 37, 49
Marincello 9
Marshall Square 81
Mission Creek 170

Mission District 53, 54, 89, 109, 150, 158, 196

Mission Dolores................................ 109

Mount Davidson............................ 79, 150, 200

Mount Sutro.. 150, 212

Muir Woods.. 9

Neiman Marcus 41

New Luneta Café 160

Nob Hill................................. 119, 121, 150, 153

Noe Valley 106, 150

North Beach......... 134, 150, 176, 178, 184, 227

Ocean Beach 38

Old Ship Saloon 55, 226

Old Spaghetti Factory........................... 184

Outside Lands................................... 38

Pacific Heights...................................... 150

Pacific Union Club.......................... 119

Palace Hotel 122, 208

Palace of Fine Arts 5, 47, 48

Panama Canal................................. 49

Park Police Station................................. 34

Pioneer Monument 81, 83

Playland at the Beach.............................. 84, 223

Point Lobos 80

Portsmouth Square 25, 142, 144

Presidio 25, 47, 58, 101, 108, 109, 133, 196, 227

Richmond District 58, 109, 150

Russian Hill.................................... 124, 150, 166

San Bruno Jail....................................... 22

San Francisco City Hall 14, 75, 77, 81, 83, 116

San Francisco General Hospital..................... 166

San Francisco–Oakland Bay Bridge 62, 193

San Quentin Prison 19, 65, 210

Seals Stadium... 27, 29

Sentinel Building. (See Columbus Tower)

Sing Chong Building................................ 25, 26

St. Francis Hotel 50, 51

St. Mary's Square................................... 191

Sue Bierman Park... 196

Sunset District 35, 150

Sutro Baths 186, 210, 212

Sutro Forest 212

Sutro Heights 212, 213

Sutro Tower 216

Sydney Walton Park 88

Tadich Grill.. 84, 204

Telegraph Hill......5, 79, 80, 95, 98, 101, 106, 107, 108, 124, 137, 150, 196, 226, 227, 228

Tenderloin 207

Teno's Barber Shop 160

The Palace of the Legion of Honor.............. 148

Third Street Bridge.................................... 152

Transamerica Pyramid............................ 11, 226

Treasure Island 142, 193, 195

Twin Peaks 89, 140, 150, 200

Union Square 35

Vaillancourt Fountain....................................... 31

V. C. Morris Building.................................. 60

War Memorial Opera House........................ 111

Washerwoman's Cove 49

Washington Square 58

Western Addition................... 86, 150, 168, 182

What Cheer House............................... 186

Woodward's Gardens....................................... 186

Yellowstone National Park 9, 22

Yerba Buena Island 193